Migrant Workers' Education in China

Adult Learning, Literacy and Social Change

SERIES EDITORS:

Anna Robinson-Pant (University of East Anglia, UK)
Alan Rogers (University of East Anglia, UK and University of Nottingham, UK)

This series explores the complex relationship between adult learning and social change. Instead of the common focus on adult literacy as kick-starting development, the series considers how adult learning and literacy can also emerge from processes of social change. Each volume introduces new theoretical and methodological lenses to investigate insights into adult learning and literacy based on original empirical research by the authors. Recognising that Governments from the Global North as well as the Global South have recently signed up to the Sustainable Development Goals, this series brings together research conducted in a wide range of countries, including Malawi, Nepal, China, the Philippines and the UK.

ADVISORY BOARD:

Dennis Banda (University of Zambia, Zambia)
Lesley Bartlett (University of Wisconsin, USA)
Maria Lucia Castanheira (Federal University of Minas Gerais, Brazil)
Mostafa Hasrati (Seneca College, Canada)
Li Jiacheng (East China Normal University, China)
Judy Kalman (CINVESTAV, Mexico)
Simon McGrath (University of Nottingham, UK)
Tonic Maruatona (University of Botswana, Botswana)
Tony Mays (Commonwealth of Learning)
Hendrik Nordvall (Mimer, The Swedish Network for Research on Popular Education, Sweden)
Mastin Prinsloo (University of Cape Town, South Africa)
Anita Rampal (University of Delhi, India)
Bonnie Slade (University of Glasgow, UK)

Also available in the series:
Literacies, Power and Identities in Figured Worlds in Malawi,
Ahmmardouh Mjaya

Forthcoming in the series:
Adult Learning and Social Change in the UK: National and Local Perspectives,
edited by Jules Robbins and Alan Rogers

Migrant Workers' Education in China

Changing Discourses and Practices

Fusheng Jia

BLOOMSBURY ACADEMIC
LONDON • NEW YORK • OXFORD • NEW DELHI • SYDNEY

BLOOMSBURY ACADEMIC
Bloomsbury Publishing Plc
50 Bedford Square, London, WC1B 3DP, UK
1385 Broadway, New York, NY 10018, USA
29 Earlsfort Terrace, Dublin 2, Ireland

BLOOMSBURY, BLOOMSBURY ACADEMIC and the Diana logo are trademarks
of Bloomsbury Publishing Plc

First published in Great Britain 2022
Paperback edition first published 2024

Copyright © Fusheng Jia, 2022

Fusheng Jia has asserted his right under the Copyright, Designs and Patents Act, 1988,
to be identified as Author of this work.

For legal purposes the Acknowledgements on p. xii constitute an extension of this copyright page.

Cover design: Charlotte James
Cover image © Vince Cavataio/Getty Images

All rights reserved. No part of this publication may be reproduced or transmitted
in any form or by any means, electronic or mechanical, including photocopying,
recording, or any information storage or retrieval system, without
prior permission in writing from the publishers.

Bloomsbury Publishing Plc does not have any control over, or responsibility for, any
third-party websites referred to or in this book. All internet addresses given in this book
were correct at the time of going to press. The author and publisher regret
any inconvenience caused if addresses have changed or sites have ceased
to exist, but can accept no responsibility for any such changes.

A catalogue record for this book is available from the British Library.

Library of Congress Cataloging-in-Publication Data
Names: Klemme, Heiner, editor. | Kuehn, Manfred, editor.
Title: The Bloomsbury dictionary of eighteenth-century German philosophers /
edited by Heiner F. Klemme and Manfred Kuehn.
Other titles: Dictionary of eighteenth-century German philosophers
Description: New York: Bloomsbury Publishing Plc, 2016. | Originally
published under title: Dictionary of eighteenth-century German
philosophers: London: Continuum, 2010. | Includes bibliographical
references and index.
Identifiers: LCCN 2015040044| ISBN 9781474255974 (pb) | ISBN 9781474256001
(epub) | ISBN 9781474255981 (epdf)
Subjects: LCSH: Philosophers–Germany–Dictionaries. | Philosophy,
German–18th century–Dictionaries.
Classification: LCC B2615.D53 2016 | DDC 193–dc23
LC record available at http://lccn.loc.gov/2015040044

ISBN:	HB:	978-1-3501-7072-8
	PB:	978-1-3502-8750-1
	ePDF:	978-1-3501-7074-2
	eBook:	978-1-3501-7073-5

Series: Adult Learning, Literacy and Social Change

Typeset by Integra Software Services Pvt. Ltd.

To find out more about our authors and books visit www.bloomsbury.com
and sign up for our newsletters.

Contents

List of Figures	vi
Series Foreword	vii
Migrant Workers' Education in China: Changing Discourses and Practices	x
Acknowledgements	xii

1	Migration and Adult Learning in China	1
2	Reflexivity, Processes and Assemblages	29
3	Exploring Different Voices in Education Policies	43
4	Exploring the Teaching Force	73
5	Exploring Pedagogical Practice	85
6	Exploring Outward Development	105
7	Examining Assessment of Students	115
8	Adult Learning Practices and Changing Subjectivities	133
9	Assemblage, Tensions and Social Change	163

Notes	177
References	179
Index	188

Figures

1.1	An industrial park near Mountainview Village, Goods Town	20
3.1	A job advertisement of an electronic factory in Goods Town	51
6.1	Outward Development organized by the Home of Migrants College	106
6.2	An outward development project with students of the Home of Migrants College	107

Series Foreword

Adult Learning, Literacy and Social Change

This series explores the complex relationship between adult learning, literacy and social change through empirical research conducted within and beyond educational programmes in a wide range of countries in the Global North and South. Since the launch of the 2030 Sustainable Development Goals, there has been growing interest in how adult literacy – sometimes referred to as 'the invisible glue' (LWG 2007) – connects the seventeen goals. Much research has focused on how to measure literacy progress quantitatively (through literacy rates) against such development indicators and assumed that most literacy learning takes place formally within institutions or educational programmes. Rather than taking this instrumental approach, this series investigates the 'why' and 'how' of the assumed relationship between adult learning, literacy and social change.

The UNESCO Chair in Adult Literacy and Learning for Social Transformation (based at University of East Anglia, UK) has strongly shaped the approach and stance of this series. Aiming to develop understanding about how adult literacy and learning – particularly for women and young adults – can help address inequalities in the poorest communities of the world, the UNESCO Chair brings together university departments specializing in adult literacy and community learning in the UK, Ethiopia, Nepal, Malawi, Egypt and the Philippines. Several of the books in this series emerged from in-depth qualitative research studies conducted by researchers within this international partnership.

Providing a much-needed critical perspective on adult literacy and development, the series challenges the usual starting point of international and national policy discourse and research in this field. First, the shift to consider social change rather than development offers a broader, holistic lens, since 'development' implies a limited perspective on social change as predetermined, planned, staged, and often with an envisaged endpoint (Castles 2001). Conceptual debate on 'social transformation' (defined as 'big' social change by Haas et al. 2020) informs this analysis – particularly the notion that 'social transformations are deeply political in nature, an insight which dominant, "technocratic" development theories and ideologies ignore and actively try to conceal' (ibid, 7). This alternative lens provides a way to step outside development frameworks that focus only on literacy and development outcomes, in order to recentre attention onto people's lived experiences of social change.

Secondly, this series is grounded on an 'ideological' rather than an 'autonomous' model of literacy (Street 1984). In contrast to much international development policy and research which has drawn on an understanding of literacy as decontextualized skills learned in a classroom, the series takes a 'situated' approach (Barton, Hamilton and Ivanic 2000) to investigate literacy and adult learning in everyday life. Researching informal and nonformal learning – both within and beyond educational institutions and development programmes – the authors offer original insights into how adults are engaging with an ever-increasing diversity of literacies, languages, cultural values and technologies. Resisting the common tendency to conflate literacy, learning and education, they explore the complex relationships around power, knowledge and identities that are shaping people's lives and social change.

Thirdly, this series accepts the now widely held view of adult learning as comprising formal, non-formal and informal elements (UNESCO 2009: 27); not necessarily as discrete activities but often inextricably mixed in a lifelong and lifewide process of interaction between social members. Learning can no longer be seen as the sole prerogative of educational institutions in time-limited activities; it takes multiple forms and occurs in multiple locations throughout life. The volumes in this series will explore how such adult learning is inspired by and at the same time contributes to social change.

As the world now grapples with the devastating effects of the global Covid-19 pandemic, climate change, conflict, migration and widening inequalities, the focus of this series is particularly relevant. More than ever before, social change is seen as unpredictable, and new educational challenges are emerging. The authors in this series do not set out to advocate solutions for policy makers or educational providers. However, these in-depth research accounts share rich first-hand experiences, observations, analysis and voices that are often unheard, thereby introducing new ways to understand adult learning, literacy and social change.

Anna Robinson-Pant
Alan Rogers

References

Barton, D., M. Hamilton and R. Ivanic (2000), *Situated Literacies: Reading and Writing in Context*, London: Routledge

Castles, S. (2001), 'Studying Social Transformation', *International Political Science Review*, 22 (1): 13–32

Haas, H., S. Fransen, K. Natter, K. Schewel and S. Vezzoli (2020), *Social Transformation*, International Migration Institute Working Papers, Paper 166, July 2020, Oxford: IMI

Street, B. V. (1984), *Literacy in Theory and Practice*, Cambridge: Cambridge University Press

University of East Anglia UNESCO Chair: https://www.uea.ac.uk/groups-and-centres/unesco-chair-programme

UK Literacy Working Group (2007), Literacy and international development: the next steps, LWG Position Paper. Available online: http://balid.org.uk/pdfs/LWG%20Position%20Paper%20Final%20June07%20CD%20final.doc

UNESCO (2009), *Global Report on Adult Learning and Education*, Hamburg: UIL

Migrant Workers' Education in China: Changing Discourses and Practices

This series sets out to explore and problematize the relationship between adult learning, literacy and social change. The second volume of the series presents a strong challenge to the dominant assumptions of a simple linear relationship between adult learning and development which have informed much international and national educational policy.

Dr Fusheng Jia conducted ethnographic research for over a year with two educational programmes established by the State for migrant workers in an economically developed province in Southern China. From his participant observation within communities and classrooms (virtual and face to face) and informal discussions with participants, policy makers and teachers, he develops a complex picture of how power hierarchies and competing ideologies were shaping these adult-learning programmes. Within this account, the voices of migrant workers are most striking and offer the reader unusually intimate insights into their frustrations and aspirations for learning and a better life. Their experiences reveal the importance of informal learning as they develop strategies to learn new skills and find or retain work: the formal and non-formal programmes provided are only one element in their educational journey. The rich ethnographic data vividly illustrates the underpinning conceptualization of adult learning in this series, as embedded in a lifelong and lifewide process of social interactions and relationships.

An important starting point of the series is the distinction between international development and social change, terms that are often conflated or used interchangeably. This book takes forward these ideas through analysing the ways in which processes of social change are intertwined with and sometimes contest development discourses within the two adult-learning programmes studied. Fusheng Jia analyses the tensions and contradictions emerging, as educational structures influenced by ideologies of collectivism were joined by new forces of commercialization. By focusing on specific educational events and practices, he provides deep analysis into the different ways in which people and institutions were engaging with changing values. An example is the 'outward development' initiative for migrant learners – a training event contracted out by the state-run Home of Migrants College to a tourism company, resulting in a contradictory mix of commercial and collective values being promoted, such as self-sacrifice, selfless devotion alongside personal development and self-promotion.

This holistic account – extending from analysis of publicity and admissions procedures to curriculum, assessment practices and employment outcomes – provides detailed evidence of how educational programmes for migrant workers can lead to greater social inequalities and marginalization. Though based on research conducted some years ago, this book has particular relevance for present-day challenges, as adult educators around the world explore how to develop online or blended learning approaches in the face of the Covid-19 pandemic. The investigation into migrant workers' experiences of interacting with each other and their teachers in the QQ Chatrooms illuminates the value of such learning, particularly for those with insecure and unpredictable lives. However, what comes across most strongly in this ethnography is Fusheng Jia's empathy for students like Liu Qiang who cherished his dream to attend a 'real university', and Jiangang, a bus driver, who joked that their programme was indeed 'watered down'. The book contributes unique insights into the complex relationship between lifelong learning and social change and leaves the reader with a sense that we too have journeyed along with the migrant learners, teachers and administrators.

Anna Robinson-Pant and Alan Rogers,
May 2021

Acknowledgements

I have received support and encouragement from different sources. To ensure the privacy of my research participants, I used pseudonyms for the institutions, the places and my research participants in relation to my fieldwork. I must thank the staff from the Home of Migrants College in Haibin City for allowing me to access their working site and observe their class activities. Without their hospitality and generosity of spirit, this research would have been on a totally different track.

I am indebted to the students in the Home of Migrants College and in Yuanda Yuanmeng Plan and to the migrant workers I interviewed in Goods Town, Lychee City.

I am fortunate to have received training in the University of East Anglia opened to interdisciplinary perspectives. I am honoured to have been linked with the UNESCO Chair in Adult Literacy and Learning for Social Transformation at the University of East Anglia, wherein I have been spiritually and intellectually enriched and empowered in the interactions with the researchers and practitioners. Thank you to Professor Anna Robinson-Pant, UNESCO Chair holder, for her invaluable academic support and theoretical ideas for my research and for close and constructive readings of my writing. Thank you to Professor Alan Rogers for his critical feedback and academic advice. Thank you to Professor Nitya Rao for always encouraging me to explore new ideas and new areas and for reading the earlier drafts of this book.

Thank you to the editors and anonymous reviewers from Bloomsbury Academic. I have tried to incorporate their suggestions, without which this book would have been presented otherwise.

1

Migration and Adult Learning in China

The origins of this book date back to 2009 when I attended some seminars in the UK higher education institutions and found people discussing 'China's rise'. This was presented as a contested topic at that time in research, for example *China Rising: Peace, Power and Order in East Asia* (Kang 2007), *China's Rise: Challenges and Opportunities* (Bergsten et al. 2009) and *China's Rise – a Threat or an Opportunity* (Yee 2011). From these studies, a mixture of sentiments such as admiration, anxiety, suspicion and hostility was easily perceived. As a Chinese citizen, I witnessed rapid changes of China from the times when rationing tickets were used for limited daily life supplies to an open and prosperous era of enormous socioeconomic development. The dividing line was the adoption of the reform and open policy in 1978. I felt proud of the achievements made by China. Meanwhile, I felt obligated to let others know some of the underpinnings for these developments. Thus, an idea struck me that I should conduct a research project on China's rural-urban migrants and their learning to present a different aspect of China.

China, as a manufacturing base, supplied industrial products for the rest of the world at the sacrifice of its own environment and natural resources. In the process of socioeconomic development, rural-urban migrant workers have played a vital role. Wen Jiabao, former Chinese Premier, stated: 'We should thank those Chinese migrant workers because they made an enormous contribution to China's modernization drive' (2009). Loyalka (2012) hailed the Chinese migrant worker as the 'unsung hero behind China's rising success on the world stage' and interpreted their courage to 'eat bitterness' as 'indomitable spirit' (5).

While globalized commercialization and international investment contributed to China's development, they impacted the traditional status and the well-being of migrant workers. In 2010, a string of eighteen suicide attempts was made, mostly by jumping from high buildings, resulting in fourteen deaths in a factory of Foxconne Technology Group, where components of mobile phones were manufactured (Moore 2012). This aroused concern from the public and social media over the world about migrant workers' working and living conditions in China. A wide range of safety measures were subsequently taken to prevent suicides. Safety nets were installed to stop workers from jumping off the buildings.

However, suicides continued with this company. In 2014, Xu Lizhi, a young migrant worker and poet, took his own life in the same way (Chen 2014). In one of his poems, Xu wrote:

> My lost time, toilsome as assembly lines,
> Packed with the latest mobile phones,
> Sold to the other side of the Ocean,
> Awaiting its next cycle.[1]

The poem described poor working conditions on assembly lines and his sense of frustration and uncertainty for his future. He represented himself as imperceptible time, integrated with the mechanical procedures of assembly lines and vanished into an unknown world.

This string of suicides made me more determined to write about migrant workers. I had experiences as a migrant both national and international. This enabled me to become sensitive to hardships and aspirations of the migrant. For instance, academic qualifications and experiences would not necessarily bring conveniences to migrants, as education embodied as certificates could be relativized and departmentalized, thus resulting in barriers to social and personal development.

To understand how adult learning was related to migrant workers' development, I conducted ethnographic fieldwork in Yuanda Province,[2] an economically developed area in south China. My fieldwork started in 2012 and lasted full time for a year. This was followed with shorter visits and online data updating. Thanks to increasingly developed digital technologies, notably modern social media, I have been able to maintain contact with my key research participants and gain new understanding of the changes in their life and occupations.

My most recent revisit to Yuanda Province was in late 2019, where I met up with some research participants. Social changes such as rapid commercializations and digitalizations were overwhelming. In the first few years of my ethnographic fieldwork, I had employed 'QQ messenger', an instantaneous communication tool, to maintain contact with my research participants. But now I noticed that this messenger was side by side with, or rather, giving way to 'WeChat', a similar software but was being widely used in commercial transactions from online shopping through taking buses to buying fruits from pedlars.

In writing this book, I have reviewed my research process and reinterpreted the events, people and discourses involved. I have realized that, over the past ten years, the major education programmes for migrant workers, where I did my ethnographic fieldwork, have been developing steadily. In recoding research themes and meanings, I have made links with current social and educational trends in a wider context. For instance, tensions and contradictions between commercialism and collectivism, as discussed in Chapters 4–6, have been constant and remain an issue for the state to resolve in an increasingly commercialized society. Thus, Xi Jinping, the president of China, stresses the necessity of the education of patriotism, collectivism and socialism in a national conference for professional representatives including education and health workers (2020). For another instance, I have reinterpreted online and face-to-face learning (Chapter 5) and multiple modes of learning – formal, informal and nonformal learning (Chapter 8). When I started my fieldwork, the blended learning format was not totally embraced. However, under the impact of the Covid-19 pandemic, multiple modes of learning have been accepted and accredited. This aligns with the UNESCO's (2020) recommendations for digital learning technology and formal, non-formal and informal learning activities to fulfil the goal of lifelong learning.

This chapter presents how migration and adult education developed in the history of the People's Republic of China. Then it introduces my fieldwork background and process. Finally, it provides the highlights of each subsequent chapter. I use government and research discourses in combination with my own experiences and reflexivity to describe state policies, migration and adult learning.

State policies and migration

After its foundation in 1949, the P.R. China controlled the surge of migration until the 1980s with the adoption of the reform and opening policy in 1978. Large-scale migration took place in the 1990s when Deng Xiaoping conducted his south China tour in 1992, clarifying marketing economy as the direction of the national development. This section reviews migration in relation to socioeconomic development in the history of the P.R. China to furnish a background for this book.

1950s to 1970s: Stagnant migration, class struggle and naturalized suffering

I was born in the middle of the 1960s to a community where people, using different accents, from all over China gathered to develop an industrial base. I came to understand how my parents migrated to Taiyuan City, Shanxi Province, from Linxian County, Henan Province, in the early 1950s. China was undergoing rapid industrialization and accumulation and subsequent rural-urban migration. There were no systematic data of the migrant population in the first three decades and mainly net migration estimates were used (Wu, H. 1994). Migrants were then called 'purposeless floating population' (*mangliu* 盲流), conveying a derogative meaning, as rural-urban migration was against the state policy of planned economy.

Under the First Five Year Plan (1953–1957), the agricultural sector was strategically arranged to provide capital accumulation for industry, notably heavy industry (Brødsgaard and Rutten 2017: 27). China established a preliminary foundation for socialist reform in agriculture and in the handicraft industries and transformed capitalist industrial and commercial enterprises into different forms of state capitalism (Wang 1989: 11). In January 1956, Peng Zhen, the then mayor of Beijing City, announced at a celebration assembly that Beijing had entered socialist society. By the end of 1956, socialist reform in agriculture, handicraft industries and capitalist industrial and commercial enterprises had been completed on a national scale (Xinhua Agency 1956).

Sector imbalances between agriculture and industry emerged, triggering growing rural-urban migration (Lardy 1983:1–2; Wu, H. 1994). Although the 1954 Constitution of the P.R. China allowed people 'freedom of residence and freedom to migrate' (the National People's Congress of the PRC 1954), the state did not encourage the surge of migration. In 1958, the household registration system (*hukou* 户口) was established; therefore, rural-urban migration came to a halt. A household registration booklet recorded the household leader, household members, birth date and place of birth. Those with rural household registration were not entitled to the benefits of the urban household registration holders, in terms of housing, medicare, pensions, education and employment. Being capital-intensive, the industrial sector was unable to absorb all the rural labour surplus (Brødsgaard and Rutten 2017: 62); consequently, the rural-urban migration remained stagnant until the end of the 1970s.

I grew up when rationing material supplies was the norm and collectivism, self-sacrifice and working hard were a strong social ethos, as Mao Zedong required that 'Our comrades keep up working hard' (1949). Such slogans as 'Be not scared by hardships or death' (*yi bu paku er bu pasi* 一不怕苦, 二不怕死) impacted the mentality of the Chinese people. Lei Feng, the image of a selfless and collectivism-orientated soldier, was erected as a role model. Mao Zedong called on the whole nation to 'Learn from Comrade Lei Feng' (1963).

In the early 1970s, I travelled with my mother to Peachland Village in Linxian County from Taiyuan City. She told me that we were 'going home'. We lived in this village for nearly two years. This provided me with a glimpse of rural society. There was no private ownership of cattle or land for farming, all publicly owned, even a persimmon tree at the east end of the village, which 'used to be ours', according to my mother. When villagers carrying farming tools greeted each other, they used a word '*shou*' (受), which literally meant 'suffer hardships' but referred to 'work'. This seemed to suggest that a mindset had been shaped accepting suffering as a natural part of their life.

Class struggle was a major discourse, stressing conflicts between the rich and the poor, the bourgeoisie and the proletariat. The slogan 'Never forget class struggles' could be seen on walls or blackboards. Once, I saw some landowners being displayed from village to village, all chained together and their hands bound at their backs, villagers assembling and watching, and the landowners humiliated and scared. This was different from the callous and spiteful image portrayed in the then movies on the population at large in conflict with the rich class. I realized that landowners were not so alien from other classes of peasants.

Constructed out of the discourses and policies, peasants were stratified into categories based on their economic conditions such as possession of land and livestock: Landlords, Rich Peasants, Middle Peasants, Poor Peasants and Workers (the State Council of the PRC 1950). Later, the target of resentment and persecution was expanded to the 'Five Evil Types' (*Heiwulei* 黑五类) in the Cultural Revolution (1966–1976): Landlords, Rich Peasants, Anti-revolutionaries, Bad Guys and Rightists (*di fu fan huai you* 地富反坏右). They were designated as representatives of evil people, ranging from the rich class through criminal offenders to political and intellectual dissidents.

However, I was more impressed with the history of Linxian County, notably its Red Flag Canal (*Hongqiqu* 红旗渠). This irrigation project was started in the early 1960s and was not completed until the early 1970s, connecting this county by Zhanghe River with Shanxi Province. Located in a mountainous area, Linxian County had suffered severe shortages of water resources for living and farming. Stories were many on tragedies due to the lack of water and disputes over water between different communities. One of them was about a bride who committed suicide out of a sense of guilt, as she accidentally spilled a bucket of water her father-in-law had collected far from home. Media used this story to show the trauma on the local people from the shortage of water to rationalize their motivation to build the Red Flag Canal. From time to time, I overheard from loudspeakers a song resounding over the mountainous village:

> Taihangshan Mountain's cut open,
> Zhanghe River comes along,
> How aspiring Linxian people,
> They've rearranged mountain and river.[3]

In 1975, my elder brother joined the Educated Youth Urban-Rural Migration (*zhishi qingnian shangshan xiaxiang* 知识青年上山下乡), a politically mobilized movement. This movement started in the late 1950s but was not implemented on a national scale until the Cultural Revolution under Mao Zedong's instruction (1968): 'Educated youth should go to the countryside and receive re-education from the peasant'. On that day when my brother set out, I saw arrays of young people in a line of trucks, which would carry them to different places, inspiring drum music played and loudspeakers shouting: 'Educated youth should go to the countryside, where you are most needed'. Three years later, the policy allowed my brother to return to the city and become employed with a state-run enterprise, as my father retired of age and left a place of employment for my brother. However, most of the young people did not return to the city until 1980 with the policy changes.

In December 1978, adopting the reform and opening policy, the state switched from class struggle to the construction of socialist modernization, loosening its administrative control on migration. In addition, enormous progress was achieved in the agricultural sector with the establishment of the household responsibility system, under which villagers contracted the village's collective land and other means of production. This practice led to a huge rural labour force, which was transformed into migration.

Socialist market economy and the rise of migration

In the early 1980s, some of my relatives came to Taiyuan City from Linxian to find temporary jobs on construction sites. Many of these projects in Taiyuan City were contracted by Linxian people, as they were said to be hard-working and had a good command of construction skills. Migrant workers were called peasant workers (*nongmingong* 农民工). They came when farming was in the slack season and went home in the harvesting season. My parents often invited migrant relatives for a catch-up. Again, they were often heard using the word '*shou*' (suffer).

From 1978 to 1992, the state prompted rural surplus labour force to find employment with local township and village enterprises. Consequently, there appeared 'the rapid development of rural industry under decentralisation and partial market relations' (Brødsgaard and Rutten 2017: 4). Meanwhile, four special economic zones were set up in the southern coastal ports in 1980, to which migrants nationwide gravitated. The state intended the special economic zones to entice foreign investors with preferential tax exemption and other flexible management measures.

However, the large-scale migration did not take place until after Deng Xiaoping's southern China Tour in February 1992 (Mallee 2000: 93), consolidating his theory on 'constructing socialism with Chinese characteristics'. This clarified the direction of a 'socialist market economy' (ibid, 93), and re-established 'central control over investment' from 1994 to 2012 (Brødsgaard and Rutten 2017: 4). Rural migration in 1990s proceeded on an unprecedented scale. The number of migrants soared from 40 million at the beginning of 1992 through 72 million in 1996 up to 94 million by 2002 (Wen, J. 2004), mainly into the Yangtse River Delta and the Pearl River Delta.

In early 2001, I joined this migration surge and transferred to a university in Shantou City in Guangdong Province. Located next to Hong Kong, this area had an excellent geographical position. Since the opening of China after 1978, Guangdong had been attracting migrant workers as well as other professionals. The influx of migrant workers drove the local economy forward rapidly. I remained employed within the state system, thus having no worries about benefits and income. However, migrant workers who held rural household registration had no access to benefits such as housing and medical care, which was restricted to the residents with local household registration. The household registration system gave rise to social and economic problems, increasing inequity between rural and urban people. As Wong, Li and Song (2007) argue, 'the "hukou" system (household registration system), the process of decentralization and the obscure role of trade unions have contributed to the experience of marginalization of rural migrant workers in urban cities in China' (34).

As I gained more understanding of migrant workers, I realized that the so-called suffering (*shou*) was not a local thought restricted to Linxian people but shared by the migrants in China (e.g. Loyalka 2012; Griffiths and Zeuthen 2014), and was a similar perception in other parts of the world, as Holmes (2013) suggests in relation to Mexican migrant workers in America

In reflecting why their suffering was naturalized, I drew on Kabeer's (1994) analysis of rules, which include discourses and ideologies such as norms, values, laws and customs (281). When fully institutionalized, rules make the way things are done appear 'natural or immutable' (ibid, 282). In addition, I gained inspiration from Holmes' (2013) observation and understanding of the naturalized suffering of Mexican migrant workers. I became aware, thereby, that the discourses around suffering could influence people, if fully immersed, that they would no longer question their suffering.

The naturalized suffering of migrant workers could be traced back to 1940s to 1950s when stratifications of peasants were conducted, and suffering was eulogized. In addition, the state and government discourses in Mao Zedong's times promoting hard work exerted an impact on people's mentality. However, not every sufferer would accept the normalization of suffering when they awoke to their suffering and enhanced their awareness of its workings.

New generation migration: Aspiration and disillusion

Since the beginning of the twenty-first century, rural-urban migration was largely on the increase. The floating population had reached 236 million by 2012, with an increase of over one hundred million over the year of 2000 (the National Health and Family Planning Commission of China 2013). However, from 2014 onwards, the migration into large cities remained stagnant, and there was almost no increase in migrant numbers in large cities (Gregory and Meng 2018: 396).

At the surge of migration, a new term '*wailaigong*' (外来工) (workers from outside) came to be used. *Wailaigong* was obviously broader in its connotations, as not every migrant worker was a peasant, and some could be highly valued professionals. However, the use of this word reduced, in a certain sense, some of the negative elements contained in *nongmingong*, the earlier saying for migrant workers.

The state addressed the migration formally and systematically by adopting comprehensive measures. The State Council of China (2006) defined rural-urban migrant workers as:

> a new type of labour force that came into being after China's reform and opening up, and China's industrialisation and urbanisation. With their household registration in rural areas, they are mainly engaged in non-agricultural industries. Some of them migrate to find employment in slack season, thus they are both industrial and agricultural workers with strong mobility. Some others are long employed in urban areas and a vital part of the industrial workforce.

Most migrant workers were born in the 1980s, thus being categorized as second-generation migrant workers. Over 60 per cent of the migrant workers were between sixteen and thirty years old (the National Bureau of Statistics of China 2010). A large-scale and comprehensive 'Research report on new generation rural-urban migrant workers' by All-China Federation of Trade Unions (2010) reveals some thought-provoking findings. According to this report, young migrant workers were eager to enhance their self-development but uncertain about their future. Seventy per cent of those under forty years of age had received junior middle school education, while 26 per cent of those aged under thirty years had received senior middle school and 31.1 per cent of those aged between 21 and 25 years had senior middle school qualifications. However, over half of the migrant workers did not receive any vocational training. The report concludes that the older generation aimed to make money for families back home and exhibited a strong ability to survive. However, the second generation, although having 'a strong sense of their own rights', often felt marginalized and emotionally fragile (All-China Federation of Trade Unions 2010).

However, with such discourses as democracy, freedom, justice and human rights becoming more and more influential among migrant workers, they learned to protect themselves and fight for better benefits. Nationwide, the gap between the rich and the poor was widening. As pointed out by Chinese president Xi Jinping, the major social contradiction in Chinese society is the discrepancy between people's increasing demand for good life and the unbalanced and insufficient development (Xi 2017). Popular discourses seemed to suggest that migrant workers contributed to the urban crisis (Zhao 2002; Sun 2020), thus constantly needing education to improve their own population quality (*suzhi* 素质) (Yan 2008). More recently, discourses of migrant workers are still around population quality such as low literacy levels, low employability and no interest in training (e.g. Wang and Chen 2021).

The state took comprehensive measures, such as launching education policies and programmes, for migrant workers. It appeared to be on the side of the discourse defining the newly formulated middle class as being a high-quality population (Anagnost 2004) and identified migrant workers as low-quality population, who needed to receive further education and training. Thus, migrants were directed to a range of education initiatives and policies, put forward in the early 2000s.

Adult learning from 1949 to 1978: Education activities and political mobilizations

In the past seven decades, state policies stressed the importance of adult education nationwide in response to economic development and social transformations. However, adult education in the first three decades, in step with state policies, required learners to be politically orientated yet well-equipped with good expertise. In addition, learning was closely related to the practice in jobs.

The extremely low literacy rate in China hindered economic development when the PRC was founded. Over 80 per cent of the Chinese population were illiterate while the illiteracy rate in rural areas was as high as 95 per cent (Yi 2019). The State Council (1951) issued a resolution on education reform, emphasized the status of adult literacy training classes and industrial and agricultural schools. Consequently, there appeared an 'expansion of worker-peasant part-time education' from 1951 to 1952 (Ascher 1976: 9). Many part-time schools for adult education were set up; 'notably, over 30,000 part-time agricultural high schools' (Ascher 1976: 19).

A series of official documents and notices in the 1950s show the central government required that adult literacy education be implemented in both urban and rural areas (Yi 2019). 'The Notice of the State Council of China on Illiteracy Elimination' in 1956 decided that the objectives of illiteracy elimination be mainly those from 14 to 50 years of age, with the literacy standard of knowing 2,000 Chinese characters for workers and 1,500 for peasants. They should read simple and popular articles in newspapers, do simple sums, write simple notes and do simple abacus calculation (ibid). The 1950s literacy campaign was 'the largest and most dramatic event in China's history' (Peterson 2001: 226).

Technical and vocational trainings were also highlighted by the central government. During the first decade of the PRC, Li, C. (1960) reports that 'On-the-job training and apprenticeship were introduced on a national scale' (40). Training assumed practicable and flexible ways. Cui (2012) recalls how Tianjin Municipal Government prescribed how the training of new workers should be conducted around 1958: the management of workshops should deliver theoretical learning and invite technicians and experienced workers to teach; a master worker (*shifu* 师傅) should be allocated to each new apprentice. This helped shape the induction and training practices of new workers for a few decades in China's industrial sector. Consequently, 'the engineering and technical personnel in industry grew from 58,000 in 1952 to 175,000 in 1957; overall, employees engaged in industrial fields grew from 6.15 million to 10.19 million' (Li, C. 1960: 40).

Education and political mobilizations were closely related, as noted by Ascher (1976), 'the ideological path and leadership of the Communist Party' was central to China's socioeconomic development (3). Mao Zedong (1957) pointed out the importance of politics in relation to business in the Third Plenary Session of the Eighth Congress of the Communist Party of China: 'Politics and business are dialectically integrated. Politics is primary and foremost. We must be opposed to any tendencies without concern about politics. However, we cannot do politics without considering business'.

Teaching methods and educational discourses show that China's literacy campaign sought to develop learners' awareness of 'the political and economic objectives of collectivization' (Peterson 2001: 227) and socialist reform in the process of literacy education. Learning enthusiasm could be often achieved by arousing resentment for those who used to be well off before the collectivization and socialist reform.

Recollections of how literacy classes were conducted in 1950s are many. For instance, Guo (2017) describes a typical day for a literacy class: the first lesson started with learners' complaints on the sufferings of illiterates; one narrated how a literate landowner made a fool of an illiterate poor peasant family. Literate landlords and illiterate poor peasants constituted a tension.

Likewise, an excerpt from a stage opera 'Husband and Wife Learning Literacy' (*fuqi shizi* 夫妻识字), appearing in the 1940s, is revealing:

Why do we peasants need to be literate?
Being illiterate, we did not know of important events.
In the old society, we were illiterate.
We were bullied unaware.
Today, we have stood up.
We used to be sufferers,
But we are our own masters now.
How can we remain illiterate?[4]

Discourses such as 'sufferers', 'masters', 'bullied' and 'stood up' in the excerpt above propelled peasants to be identified with the class of sufferers, evoking hostility and hatred for those with wealth and influence. This practice in combination with literacy education developed peasants' awareness of class divisions among themselves and contributed to their changing identities.

The intertwined relationship between political mobilization and education reached a climax in the 1966–1976 Cultural Revolution. In 1966, Mao Zedong, in his 'May the 7th Instruction' (*wuqi zhishi* 五七指示), called on students to integrate academic education with industry, agriculture and military study. He required 'the education duration to be shortened' and 'education to be revolutionised', so that 'the phenomenon of the bourgeoisie swaying our schools cannot continue' (ibid). Students, who formed Red Guards (*hongweibing* 红卫兵) and were joined by the population at large, were mobilized for a ten-year long nationwide political struggle against the so-called representatives of the bourgeoisie within the Communist Party of China.

University entrance exams were cancelled; instead, recruitment of university students was based on the principle of 'expression of interest from student candidates, recommendation from grassroots masses, approval by supervisors and auditing by education providers' (Zhang, Ding and Wu 2021). This was intended to unite the masses of workers and peasants and provide opportunities for the working class. This idea was vividly and dramatically reflected in the movie *Breaking* (1975) (*Juelie* 决裂). This movie, directed by Li Wenhua (李文化), was produced by Beijing Film Studio in 1975. Contextualized in Jiangxi Province in the late 1950s, this motion picture reflects contradictions of different understandings and practices in running adult higher education. Although some believe that the university should be aimed for elite students with better literacy skills, people of positive images represented by Long Guozheng 龙国正, a high-rank official of this university, attributed low literacy skills of student candidates to the impact from the old unfair society, where workers and peasants were deprived of schooling opportunities, thus being exploited by the class of landlords and capitalists. He argues that adult higher education should be open to the masses of workers and peasants and low literacy restrictions on student candidates should be shaken off. In this movie, when Jiang Danian 江大年, a blacksmith, was not able to be accepted for admission to the university due to his low literacy level,

Long Guozheng challenged this decision. He passionately raised Jiang Danian's callused hand, announcing to the public that this hand was his eligibility for the university education.

However, such stories reflecting young people from working class, such as Jiang Danian, achieving upward social mobility through university education, did not always happen in a realistic setting. In fact, this method of student recruitment resulted in severely corrupt practices, as it stifled qualified talents and excluded the children of the ordinary masses (Sun, J. and Hao, M. 2019). It also deprived of education opportunities many young people who had relatives categorized into the 'Five Evil Types', as stated earlier in this chapter.

Towards the end of the 1970s, as the state switched from class struggle to economic development, the connection between political mobilization and education was declining.

The past four decades: HE fervour and migrant education

The university entrance exam (*gaokao* 高考) was restarted in December 1977. This aroused people's enthusiasm and obsession with higher education academic qualifications. Gaokao was an opportunity for rural household registration holders to become urban citizens if they were admitted to a university. It also established a platform for the children of the 'Five Evil Types' through which to be promoted through their own talents and efforts. Competition was extremely fierce.

In 1981, the state opened higher education programmes for part-time adult education. This produced opportunities for those who could not gain access to full time higher education. Meanwhile, the state launched policies for enhancing workers' techniques and literacy levels. In the late 1980s, I started teaching with a university in Taiyuan City. I was also assigned to teaching English to adult students working part-time towards degrees in engineering courses. The students were mostly employees from some state-run enterprises, which formulated partnerships with my university and established teaching centres in their cities. This shows that the education policies, especially those concerning higher education programmes for adult education, mainly benefited those who had already entered the state system such as large-scale enterprises and public sector. For many years afterwards, adult learning in rural areas remained overlooked. Over-enthusiasm with higher education qualifications became a social issue.

To curb the blind fervour with academic degrees, the Ministry of Education of China issued a notification in 1987, which required adult education be focused on those employed with enterprises to promote their technical skills and literacy levels. This document also pointed out major problems in adult education including 'disconnection between adult learning and social needs, mismatches between learning methods and contents and the features of adult education' (ibid). Even so, the pursuit of university education and a higher academic degree has remained an endeavour for many Chinese people from then on.

The government had not addressed migrant workers' education until the twenty-first century. As stated above, current migrant workers had richer formal education experiences than the first-generation migrant workers. However, most of these migrant workers did not receive appropriate vocational training. Both central and local government became aware of this issue and made a series of education policies.

The epochal one was the '2003-2010 China's rural-urban migrant workers training plan', which aimed to 'enhance the population quality of migrant workers and their employability and further contribute to a transfer of the rural labour force to non-rural industries in urban areas' (the State Council of the PRC 2003). This plan was intended to establish a well-equipped comprehensive continuing educational system requiring the collaborative capital investment among enterprises, government and individual migrant workers. It was designed to offer guidance and training on the issues such as knowledge of the law, common sense for urban life, protection of basic rights and hunting for jobs, and on vocational training according to different jobs (ibid).

In 2004, a few national education projects focused on peasants or migrant workers were launched by the ministries of central government, such as the 'Sunshine training project for rural labour force diversion' (the Ministry of Agriculture of the PRC 2004) and 'Training plan for rural labour force diversion' (the Ministry of Education of the PRC). To further stress the importance of the learning and training of migrant workers, the State Council of the PRC announced 'Some guidelines on resolution of issues of migrant workers' in 2006. 'To meet the needs of increasing industrialization, urbanization and transference of rural labour surplus force', this plan required all provinces to 'develop large scale technical and vocation training for migrant workers to enhance their capacity for labour transference and adaptation to working outside' (ibid). Education was thus expected to develop migrants' capacity for survival and propel the ongoing urbanization and industrialization.

During the economic crisis in 2008, many migrant workers returned to their home villages. The State Council of the PRC (2008) issued a notice calling on local vocational education institutions to organize the vocational training of the returned migrant workers. In 2010, the State Council of the PRC reiterated this issue in its 'Guidelines on the training of migrant workers' which acknowledged 'the remarkable achievement in the training of migrant workers' while addressing such problems as 'lack of coordinated planning in training programmes, inadequate efficiency in funding utilisation, low quality in training and imperfect monitoring mechanism'.

National education policies and projects seemed to be designed and planned for utilitarian rather than transformative purposes, as they were launched to respond to changing socioeconomic conditions so that migrants could be adapted to new urban circumstances. In the 1950s, adult learning was guided onto an ideological path and instilled with the awareness of peasants having stood up as one's own 'master'. Thus, there was no clear boundary between taking adult education as a function and as a way of mobilizing masses. When the Cultural Revolution broke out, ultraleftism predominated and education became an area of political struggle. However, in the context of rapid industrialization after espousing reform and opening policy, the state encouraged migrant workers to enhance their population quality (*renkou suzhi* 人口素质) by taking education and training courses to serve for urban areas and contribute to urbanization. These education policies and their designs appeared to have deemed migrant workers to be deficient in education and technical and vocational training. The adoption of such 'deficient' discourses could legitimatize the fact that migrant workers assumed jobs requiring low population quality. Murphy (2004) believes that the use of 'population quality' as a development discourse could provide support for the state to shift its responsibility for peasants' livelihoods and collective welfare to the peasants themselves and their learning practices.

More recently, there have been research studies arguing for engaging multiple stakeholders to enhance the quality of migrant workers. Pi (2018) suggests adopting the shared governance integrating multiple stakeholders – the government, enterprises, migrant workers and education providers. Wang and Chen (2021) seem to support this stance, thereby raising some suggestions such as making systematic training plans, calling on multiple stakeholders to raise funding, and developing migrant workers' learning awareness.

So there was a change in state discourses, as the suffering discourse, as mentioned earlier, was related to self-sacrifice while the discourse around quality was associated with life aspirations in urban settings (Griffiths and Zeuthen 2014: 149). This change prompted me to problematize the issue of training policies for migrant workers and focus on the relationship and gap between education policies and migrant workers' needs and aspirations. I was concerned to explore how state education policies on migrant workers experienced changes in the process of their implementation, and how far continuing education of rural migrant workers has contributed to their aspirations and ideas of development.

I decided to conduct my research in Yuanda Province in south China, as mentioned earlier. This province was a major area of international investment, attracting migrant workers nationwide. In this book, I have examined two *Yuanmeng* 圆梦 (Dream Fulfilment) education plans for migrant workers from the perspective of understanding the process and practice of policymaking and teaching. This book has brought together policy makers, education practitioners and migrant workers as learners into dialogue and raised questions around voice and participation that were essential to address. It has explored what discourses and practical transformations occurred in the process from policy making to policy implementation.

Emergence of the Yuanmeng plans in Yuanda Province

To respond to the education policies of the central government, the Yuanda Provincial Government issued 'Modernity education construction guidelines for 2004-2020'. This document covered both formal education and vocational education, ranging from primary to tertiary level. It stressed the harmonious development of vocational education and formal senior middle school, and encouraged cooperation from industries, enterprises and society in running vocational training. It planned to establish a lifelong educational network covering the whole society.

To investigate adult education in Yuanda Province, I googled and came across the Yuanda Y*uanmeng* Plan, which literally means Dream Fulfilment Plan. However, I was unable to access its teaching sites, though I contacted its administration offices via emails, phone calls and personal visits to a Yuanmeng office in Goods Township Government, Lychee City. I contacted some teaching sites through the clues presented on websites. Then an online declaration about 'the Yuanmeng Plan' struck me that the Haibin Yuanmeng Plan was much earlier than the Yuanda Yuanmeng Plan.

In 2008, 'Haibin City General Trade Union Yuanmeng Plan educational assistance action for needy and migrant workers' was launched by the Haibin General Trade Union (shortened to the Haibin Yuanmeng Plan in this book) and focused on migrant workers in Haibin City in the first instance and later, included local household register holders.

In 2011, the Yuanda Communist Youth League initiated 'Yuanda Province new generation industrial leading workers' training and development plan' (shorted to the Yuanda Yuanmeng Plan). Sponsored by Yuanda Provincial authorities, the Yuanda Yuanmeng Plan was implemented in major cities including Haibin City. It launched its trial practice at the end of 2010 when Beijing Lakeview University was the only partnership institution, and 100 students were admitted. Thereafter, this programme has been developing so that myriad higher educational institutions have joined in this programme. In 2020, the participating colleges and universities are forty-three in total, located inside and outside Yuanda Province.

Multi-sited ethnography

Reviewing policies and national events in adult learning and development, I noticed there was a discrepancy between the images constructed out of discourses and the practices related to these discourses, such as the one between the Landowners represented as merciless in discourses and the Landowners humiliated in public. Therefore, to study the continuing education and development of migrant workers situated in the extremely mobile society engaging with various discourses, any isolated method could not portray a holistic picture. I chose to adopt an ethnographic approach to examine this issue in an exploratory way.

I aligned myself with Wacquant (2003), who describes an ethnographer as someone who conducts 'social research based on the close-up, on the-ground observation of people and institutions in real time and space' in an attempt to 'detect how and why agents on the scene act, think and feel the way they do' (5). Bryman suggests for ethnographers: being 'immersed in a social setting for an extended period time', 'observing behaviour, listening to what is said in conversations both between others and with the fieldworker, and asking questions' (Bryman 2004: 292–3). This encouraged me to be fully immersed in Yuanda Province and examined the education programmes focused on rural migrant workers, the Yuanmeng plans.

However, with increasingly developed digital technologies, I was able to be located where virtual spaces and actual spaces were interconnected and interpenetrating. This did not separate me from my research participants; on the contrary, it enabled me to be in closer contact with them in a sense.

Experiences in Lychee City, Yuanda Province

In seeking where to conduct my fieldwork in the early 2012, I encountered the Yuanda Yuanmeng Plan through its official website. I decided to base myself in Goods Town, Lychee City for two reasons. Firstly, Lychee City was said to be a centre of the world's manufacturing industry, where gathered migrant workers while Goods Town was clustered with enterprises making or processing industrial products like shoes, electronic products, computer accessories, leather products and machinery parts. Secondly, the Yuanda Yuanmeng Plan was conducted intensively in Lychee City, shown from its official website. For half a year before my fieldwork, I had had access to QQ online chat with students and staff in this programme. To my surprise, in the first round of students, around one-third of them were based in Lychee City.

I had never been to this city before. This was a bold move, but I thought I would be able to observe more from the perspective of an outsider. Towards the end of September 2012, I landed in Goods Town, Lychee City. I changed my dwelling places a few times and settled in an apartment building. There was a multitude of small- or medium-sized factories in the neighbourhood. There were also industrial giants such as Sum Sung and Nokia, and real estate developments around, where an expanse of buildings, high or low, reached far into distance.

In Goods Town, like other towns in Lychee City, there was a high percentage of land from villages let out or sold out for the purposes of real estate development or manufacturing sites. Mountainview Village, where I lived, connected other villages, forming a cluster of villages. There was not much land left for farming, but only buildings of high density. On the inner side of this village, the buildings were intended for local villagers to live in, which looked better planned while all the other parts seemed to have been randomly developed except for some main roads.

On the land sold or let to real estate developers and manufacturers, products of various kinds were made and then exported to places all over the world. With living, working, sales, authorities, locals and outsiders, different accents, and everything else integrated into one, a community was established along with many industrial parks, where factories and workshops were set up, and let to manufacturers, who made shoes, processed leather, produced paper, etc. (see Figure 1.1).

Figure 1.1 An industrial park near Mountainview Village, Goods Town, 2012. Taken by the author of this book

A few months later, I became familiar with the research settings, kept updated on the implementation of the Yuanda Yuanmeng Plan and interviewed governmental officials and migrant workers in Goods Town, Lychee City, including factory workers engaged in manufacturing, security guards for property management and migrant workers in the service industry like hairdressers and small stall owners. The data I collected included interview transcriptions, informal conversations, documents and fieldnotes of participant observation. By focusing on the events and social actors living and working around Mountainview Village, I sought to understand how far continuing education of migrant workers was related to their living and working environment. Of the migrant workers in Goods Town I interviewed, none of them had heard of the Yuanda Yuanmeng Plan.

Searching for a fieldwork site was a lengthy process. I had intended to observe on-the-job training. However, when I tentatively contacted people responsible in some enterprises, I never received any replies. I also conducted a few interviews with different vocational training centres or institutions, where I went to visit without prior appointment, to gain general information about what programmes were going on. I was surprised to find that some free development programmes for migrant workers under the title of 'Yuanmeng' Plan or other titles existed only in name on the websites but did not offer actual courses.

In addition, I sent emails to provincial-level officials in charge of the Yuanda Yuanmeng Plan, soliciting advice and permission to access their teaching sites, but unable to receive responses. Therefore, I decided to visit Goods Town Government and was received by relevant administrators. I was offered some leaflets and then referred to their official website, as they were not able to provide me with further assistance.

Gradually, what used to appear fragmented about the Yuanda Yuanmeng Plan in Lychee City became clear. As other cities in Yuanda Province had started their 2012–2013 student recruitments, Lychee City postponed its practice time and again, and changed their recruitment methods. Lychee Waterfront University was designated as the only institution for the 2012–2013 academic year in Lychee City. This brought a lot of inconveniences to student candidates, which meant that they could not take entrance exams until 2012 October, and it would be uncertain when they were able to gain access to their formal learning.

So I contacted some other institutions offering 'Yuanmeng' courses in Lychee City and found that their teaching was conducted online and face-to-face teaching time was sparingly allocated. In March 2013, I found, through an online chat with a student sponsored by the Yuanda Yuanmeng Plan, that there had been another partnership institution in Lychee City engaged in the Yuanda Yuanmeng Plan which offered face-to-face teaching. This college was Lychee Seabreeze Academy. The Yuanda Yuanmeng Plan courses in the charge of this academy were started earlier in 2011.

I visited Lychee Seabreeze Academy the next day. Surfing on its website, I learned that there had been face-to-face teaching for the Yuanda Yuanmeng Plan students, but not many teaching hours, as most subjects were conducted online except for subjects concerning education in thought and politics.

Lychee Seabreeze Academy was an educational institution that was privately owned and commercially operated. Locating its whereabouts was not easy, as it was overshadowed in towering buildings. Across the road was Lychee Waterfront University. I entered its courtyard. No security guards stopped and queried me, unlike other institutions. There was only one building as its teaching site. Acting as an agent for online teaching institutions both in and out of Yuanda Province, Lychee Seabreeze Academy provided courses ranging from undergraduate to master's degree and a range of services for universities and learners.

I asked to see a person responsible and was showed to a Mr. Chen. I told him my identity and briefly explained my purpose for this visit. He did not appear interested in getting involved with an outsider. I tried to raise as many questions as possible regarding their educational practices, fearing there would be no second chance, and I received a detailed explanation. I tentatively inquired if I could conduct observations of their teaching. He smirked incredulously, suggesting that I go to Lychee Waterfront University across the road: 'You know they are taking over this programme now'.

As Lychee Waterfront University would not start its teaching for the 2012–2013 academic year until April 2013, I decided to focus on the Haibin Yuanmeng Plan for my ethnographic research. Meanwhile, I chose to follow up the Yuanda Yuanmeng Plan online and take this programme as a virtual study case.

Fieldwork with the Home of Migrants College

I conducted participant observation of the Haibin Yuanmeng Plan from October 2012 to July 2013. I had not been able to learn of this programme until after my arrival in Lychee City. One day in October 2012, I surfed onto a website of a 'new' 'Yuanmeng' sponsored by the Haibin General Trade Union. There were thousands of students being registered at that time. They offered degree courses as well as a range of short-term vocational courses. I contacted them by email and received prompt feedback from Xiao Zhiyuan, my gatekeeper, who warmly welcomed me to visit the Home of Migrants College.

In October 2012, I thus began my fieldwork in the Home of Migrants College. Surrounding it was a multitude of businesses and services such as printing, restaurants, and clothes processing and selling. The Home of Migrants College was on the fourth and fifth floors of a building, which was the property of the Haibin Trade Union, but the first three floors were let to other companies. Xiao Zhiyuan came out to greet me. In his early 30s, Xiao appeared friendly and passionate. He introduced me to his colleagues, all women except him, all hustling and bustling, as students' resit exams would start in a few minutes.

During our lunch, Xiao Zhiyuan told me that their college began to be the only Yuanmeng partnership institution from 2008 onwards. It was several years later that Yuanda Provincial Government launched a similar campaign. Xiao was interested in my project, saying his leaders 'encouraged us to reflect on our own work in education of migrant workers'.

Thus, I gained my access to this college. Starting with Xiao Zhiyuan, I came to know more and more informants by a snowballing approach within this fieldwork site. Over the weekdays, the teaching site was occupied by full-time vocational students but utilized by migrant workers for the weekends. I was assigned to 'the Workers' Education Department', whose director was Xiao Zhiyuan. Its staff were administrators, though some of them provided teaching for weekend students.

Two months was left for the first semester of the 2012–2013 academic year. I observed a few classes on bachelors' degree courses and short-term courses. A couple of weeks later, I became familiar with the settings. I was interested in all courses offered by this college, so I went to observe a wide range of classes. I let my identity as a researcher be known to others. However, not every staff member knew me spontaneously. So, I asked for their oral consent before observing their teaching. I did not feel I was always welcomed by all the staff. I wandered from one class to another, occasionally with a sense of guilt as if I were a spy searching for secrets. Therefore, I came to focus on some staff members for observations who felt comfortable with me.

At last, I decided to follow up a short-term course on property management and household service, as the students and the teacher were very approachable. Over thirty students in this class, they took this course in preparation for an examination which would certify them as managers or directors of property management. I stayed with them for over a month, two long days each weekend. I conducted classroom observation, individual interviews and extracurricular lunch where I could talk with them freely. I also had a group discussion with the instructor and another four students. Simultaneously, I followed up their communication in an online chatroom. Winter vacation came. The school was on holiday from the middle of January to February 2013.

I then went back to the Home of Migrants College, and conducted participant observation and conducted interviews with administrators, teachers and students, kept active in their online chat rooms and collected documents concerning policy making and course and assessment design. Class open meetings, where tutors and students discussed curricular and extracurricular issues, were very informative.

However, mere observations of teaching did not contribute to my understanding of the working rules and education practices. I appeared to be over-inquisitive about something irrelevant to me. So, when Xiao Zhiyuan asked me if I would like to teach general English to the Economic Management Class and the Machinery Engineering Class, as they would be happy to have someone coming back from abroad to join their team, I immediately accepted this invitation. This move fitted Fetterman's (1998: 143) suggestion of 'reciprocity' to strengthen the relationship between the researcher and the researched.

To understand my obligations, I attended a meeting with key administrators responsible for degree courses: Chen Yi, Zhou Li, Zhao Daming and Xiao Zhiyuan, who offered me suggestions and requirements ranging from class attendance registration through assignment giving and marking to assessment of students. Thus, I started to find my positionality flowing and sliding between being a teacher and a researcher. I was able to access more of the college resources and felt more confident to raise queries without feeling guilty than when I was an observer.

For this term, there were two subjects for the Economic Management Class and three for the Machinery Engineering Class, English being one of them. Their degree-awarding body was Beijing Skyline University. The Home of Migrants College also had some other partnership institutions awarding degrees to their students. As the Economic Management Class (146 students registered) was much larger than the Machinery Engineering Class (63 students registered), the former involved distance-learning technology for the implementation of its teaching activities. Teaching was conducted simultaneously over four teaching sites. I conducted face-to-face teaching with around eighty students on the main site in the Home of Migrants College. The rest of them, connected with us via video, convened on another three sites arranged by three large-sized enterprises, as those students were mostly employees with these enterprises. The students in this class were full of initiative, compared to those in the Machinery Engineering Class. They were eager to share their experiences with me and invited me to their extracurricular activities. I thus worked with these two classes until the end of my fieldwork.

Overview of the book

Chapter 2 presents my reflections on how I conducted my fieldwork. I do not introduce step by step the research methods which I used: participant observation, in-depth interview, writing fieldnotes, document collection and data analysis. A mechanical introduction to these could break the coherency of my narrative. Instead, I present some reflections on how my research unfolded, adapted and completed so that the reader could be immersed in this narrative and analysis process. I consider as inseparable oneness the relationship of the researcher and the researched, the outside and the insider, and my prior knowledge and my theoretical lenses. The research itself was a process in which I negotiated in social practices and discourses and gaining new subjectivities. I recall how my reflexivity was flexibly utilized in the whole process from literature to data selection and analysis. I describe my dilemmas in ethics, arguing that research ethics established need to be flexibly adapted to the specific research contexts. Discrepancies in the research plan and research processes strengthened the idea that research focus be put on the research processes rather than the insider/outsider polarizations. I explain how I was guided by the concepts of the development as discourse, the Social-Relations Framework, and the concept of assemblage.

Chapter 3 examines education programmes for migrant workers in Yuanda Province in terms of their policy design, funding resources, students' recruitment and the dynamics of power relations. It aims to explore how education policy for migrant workers transformed in its implementation. This chapter attempts to listen to different voices and bring into dialogues multiple social actors including policy makers, education practitioners and migrant workers to present different understandings and perceptions of the education policies and programmes targeted at migrant workers.

Chapter 4 analyses how education projects engaged a wide range of teaching force from different sources and explores the relationships formulated between them. The way that the teaching force was arranged in the Home of Migrants College indicates that it had attempted to maintain the balance between utilizing its own staff and external professionals. This chapter shows that, while authorities attempted to align the teaching staff to dominating socialist ideology such as collective welfare and selfless devotion, some teaching staff seemed to have been more impacted by liberal marketing and commercialism. Thus, a dynamic relation between educational authorities and the teaching force seemed to have been shaped.

Chapters 5–7 explore how the education policies and programmes for migrant workers were implemented. They focus respectively on curricular practice, extracurricular activities and assessment of students. They examine the hidden ideology embedded to examine the tensions and contradictions between these education plans and their practices. Chapter 5 focuses on how curricular practice was conducted and investigates the tensions embedded between online teaching and face-to-face teaching, between interactive teaching promotion and its actual practice, and between rigid and lenient attendance registrations. Chapter 6 studies the extracurricular activities of the Home of Migrants College. It describes how an outward development project was implemented and uncovered the tensions between commercialism and collectivism embedded within this implementation process. Chapter 7 investigates how the assessment of students was conducted in the Home of Migrants College in an attempt to expose the complex relationships, the commercial practices and constant negotiations amid stakeholders in the assessment process.

Chapter 8 addresses how far continuing education of migrant workers has contributed to their aspirations and livelihood. This chapter provides an in-depth analysis of the relationship between migrant workers' learning and their changing identities. It analyses the limitations of the discourse of 'knowledge changes fate'. It lends support to the idea that adult learning integrates informal and formal learning. It also analyses how multiple forms of knowledge interacted with social connections, social rules and some other dimensions.

As a concluding chapter, Chapter 9 develops the main research findings and draws out policy implications from this book. It exposes that adult education could increase stratification of migrant workers. In addition, education qualifications served as a tool of ideological control on migrant workers. This chapter summarizes the major tensions and contradictions that existed between ideological control and commercialized practices, between curriculum design and its practice, between the discourses on knowledge and other dimensions related to aspirations and success.

I endeavour to portray and analyse how education programmes for migrant workers in China were implemented to understand the perceptions and responses to education policies and practices from educational stakeholders. I attempt to analyse on both macro and micro levels to present a holistic picture from policy making to minute events. I wish to uncover the mechanisms of how heterogeneous factors such as rules and resources were connected to drive forward educational and social development. Through this book, I hope that the reader would gain new understanding of migrant workers in China, in terms of their learning and development, their contributions, hardships and aspirations.

2

Reflexivity, Processes and Assemblages

I started my fieldwork by utilizing online events, as stated in Chapter 1, while making tentative connections with institutions, as I had thought only a physical connection was real. Later, I gained access to the Home of Migrants College.

Although I had a detailed research plan, I found the fieldwork different from expected. The research journey involved frustration and anxiety from such factors as physical fatigue from travelling over multiple sites and spatial disorientations in a strange area, reminding that my body and my mind could not be separated. In a poor physical state, I felt mentally drained. Once, Wen Xiangyang, a student from the Home of Migrants College, asked me, 'Why not get settled and live a stable life?' Wen Xiangyang, in his early twenties, was from Anhui Province, east China. In his compassionate eyes, I seemed to see my exhausted figure. I became aware that, while observing, I was also being observed.

This understanding resonated with the changing ontological and epistemological aspects of ethnography. I was not making a purely objective observation, as suggested by Malinowski (1922) for anthropology, but was involved in an interplay between subjectivities. The researcher is no longer 'objective, value-free and neutral but having a subjectivity and a positionality, that is, a social, cultural, political and economic location' (Jackson 2006: 534). Utilization of subjectivities (e.g. Ellen 1984) could play a dynamic role in research. As a researcher, I was influencing my research participants, who, in turn, were exerting their impact on me, changing the trajectory of my research process.

I found myself in constant negotiations in a few dualisms: prior knowledge and theoretical lenses, plans and events, researcher and researched, and an outsider and an insider. I became engaged in the processes and tensions where lay these dualisms and gained new understanding of these tensions and processes as well as social relationships embedded within.

Reflexivity and positionality

As subjectivities were playing a role in my research processes, researchers' reflexivity has been stressed, as 'we act in the social world and yet are able to reflect upon ourselves and our actions as objects in that world' (Hammersley and Atkinson 2007: 18). In my research, I maintained close contact with social actors such as educators, migrant workers, ordinary citizens and officials. In this process, my reflexivity influenced my respondents as well as my research trajectory. As Wright and Nelson (1995: 48) summarize, reflexivity establishes a relationship between researchers with their research objects so as to achieve 'an understanding of how identities are negotiated, and how social categories, boundaries, hierarchies and processes of domination are experienced and maintained'. In other words, my reflexivity helped establish multiple and changing relationships in research settings and was presented in different relationships and different contexts.

My identities assumed multiple and dynamic forms from different perspectives. The key point related to the dichotomy between insider and outsider, and between me and my research participants. In the Home of Migrants College, I was aware that I assumed two identities: an instructor of English and a researcher. Being the former, I must obey the rules of this school as well as of the degree-awarding university; being the latter, I must abide by the rules required of a researcher. While in the case of the Yuanda Yuanmeng Plan, most of the time being a virtual study, I found my identities fluid and unstable with equally fluid research participants, thus I attempted to use more flexible expressions to describe myself. This was a reconciling process in which I ensured the clarity of my overt research while unfolding my purpose and identity.

My reflexivity determined I would share with readers 'how much of what by whom'. This meant that not all the social actors would be treated equally in my analysis and narrative. McNess, Arthur and Crossley (2013) suggest examining the role of the researcher in a hierarchical relationship, as 'we could do more to interrogate the nature of the power of the researcher' (310). This directed me to query my position as a writer.

I employed ethnographic research methods including participant observation, in-depth interview, writing fieldnotes, document collection and data analysis. I developed a reflexive approach to my research. For instance, I needed to translate large amounts of data such as interview scripts and documents from Chinese into English. Adopting a reflexive stance, I combined my experiences with the mainstream and research discourses in representing the history of rural-urban migration in China, the learning of migrant workers and the changes in their life and aspirations.

In addition, as a researcher, I might have shown more sympathy with migrant workers and taken a more critical attitude towards education providers, as I had more contact with the former. This could have generated biases towards the latter. As explored in Chapter 5, 'interactive' teaching in the Home of Migrants College had been prescribed in its curriculum, while its actual teaching was not always interactive with every teacher. However, I cited myself reflexively as a teacher who was not able to be interactive enough in this programme. So, I became one of the teaching staff criticized by myself as a researcher. This reflexive move relieved me of a sense of guilt.

In these recurrent and overlapping processes, my identities shifted and slid between being a researcher and an instructor, or between a researcher and a translator.

Negotiations in research ethics

As my ethnographic research was on continuing education in relation to aspirations and perceptions of migrant workers, I had wide connections with social actors. Therefore, I would be careful, when generating knowledge, not to harm my research participants in any way. To achieve this wish, I, as a researcher, was always reminding myself to be conscious of the ethical practice codes in ethnography established for researchers.

Firstly, to ensure the privacy of research participants and research fieldwork sites, I used pseudonyms for all research participants, institutions and places involved in my fieldwork in line with the practice of anonymity. As an observer, I might be more sensitive to certain points that would arouse conflicts between research participants. So, to protect my research participants, I had deleted some data, which could be controversial. Otherwise, as Fetterman (1998) says, 'The delicate web of interrelationships in a neighbourhood, a school or an office' 'might be destroyed' (142).

In addition, I followed Fetterman's (1998: 143) suggestion for 'reciprocity' to strengthen the relationship between the researcher and the researched. To carry out this idea, for example, I accepted the invitation by the Home of Migrants College to teach students English and I actively joined their virtual chat rooms to promote their learning enthusiasm. For another example, I did some assistance work for my interviewees. Yin Fa, as cited in Chapter 8, established friendship with me. As he ran a small stall business, I would do assistance work for him when he was busy. This could be a remedy for the time he lost for my presence.

However, I found the ethical rule on informed consent required of a researcher like me was sometimes not easy to follow. It could be even pressurising in some cases. In my fieldwork, I normally asked for consents, especially conducting individual interviews. I was usually able to acquire only oral consent. General responses were, 'you just interview us if you like. There is no need to sign a formal consent form'. I also observed this rule when doing online interview. For instance, in gaining access to the Yuanda Yuanmeng Plan, I first engaged myself in virtual spaces set up by some teaching sites. Although it was a virtual forum, I let my identity and my purpose be known to the public. People could misunderstand my intention and embarrassing events did happen. In one virtual forum, I was kicked out, as the administrator said that I was 'doing advertisement for foreign educational institutions'.

In the case of the Haibin Yuanmeng Plan, I received similar responses to my research consent advice. When I explained to my gatekeeper, Xiao Zhiyuan, that I would need his agreement by giving a signature on a consent form, as this was our academic requirement, he hesitated a moment and then laughed good naturedly to conceal his embarrassment, saying it would be all right that he did not sign it, as 'we have had some emails', which indicated his agreement. As Chinese, I understood that people did not have a strong sense of informed consents for research interview. To sign one's name on a piece of paper such as a consent form was often associative of unnecessary responsibility rather than a way of reassurance.

On reflection, I had been attempting to solicit a consent form from my research participants. However, this was mainly out of a respect for the established ethical rule. I was also obliged to do so, as a researcher with the UK university, which was a legal requirement. However, I could have used more of my reflexivity and been more explicit about my research purposes, processes and possible outcomes. This would have relieved those involved in research of any anxiety over any subsequent responsibilities to establish rapport and cooperation.

Researcher and researched as oneness

Doing ethnographic research involved a constant negotiation between I, as a researcher, and the researched. This was a process in which both parties came to achieve understanding and cooperation.

The Yuanmeng plans were large-scale top-down education programmes initiated by the government, but there seemed to be no adequate systematic measures or plans for the evaluation of these programmes conducted by independent research institutions or projects. In the Haibin Yuanmeng Plan, evaluation practices included end of term students' feedback, reports and briefings on authorities' inspection, collection of leaders' speeches, and reflections of alumni students and the staff. Obviously, the Home of Migrants College was interested in immediate assessment results from such tools as questionnaires and quantitative research.

Xiao Zhiyuan, my gatekeeper, once said to me: 'You seem to be interested in observing and recording what you see and what is happening' (Online interview notes with Xiao Zhiyuan, 03/05/2013). What he implied seemed to be that I would not give a clear response or solution to migrant workers' problems. I believed that he was worried if my research project would ever be completed if I just continued observing, as he suggested to me more than once: 'You could give out some questionnaires to students. This would be easier for you'. This showed that many people did not understand my research approach, by which I prolonged my activities and observations in an institution.

Interestingly, I was not the only one who conducted research in the Home of Migrants College. Once I encountered a researcher distributing questionnaires to my students, collecting them in half an hour and leaving soon. Some of my students, in a reassuring way, told me that they would also be happy to answer my questionnaires if I had any. That did encourage me more than amused me, as I was at a loss for what to do next and what data I had acquired to be of relevance. I accumulated much data, but I did not know which of them would be useful. So towards the end of my fieldwork in the Home of Migrants College, I designed a questionnaire for this project and distributed them to my students. They did it accordingly while whispering to each other: 'Let's make it a good one. It is not easy for our teacher'. This experience illuminated me that the students were not the targets of being gazed and researched only, but they had become a natural and collaborative part of my research.

Questionnaires or other assessment measures that yielded immediate results seemed to be popular with both the staff and the students. It was not easy to put across to the staff or even the students the importance of ethnographic approach. Robinson-Pant (2000) has stated the difficulties in making 'ethnographic research findings' communicable 'in a government programme where staff are used to more top-down administrative and planning structures' (157). However, my experiences with the Home of Migrants College, different from rigid quantitative questionnaires, showed how education stakeholders, such as education providers and migrant workers as students, produced their thoughts and implemented their plans dynamically in a natural setting.

As a result, as a researcher, I had formulated a strong relationship with the researched, as both being a natural and collaborative part of the research process. I was able to exchange ideas and participate in social events with those involved in my research, both contributing to the development of the research project. My research follows this strand to expose various tensions, contradictions and processes, where research meaning resides and where an ethnographer like me constantly gains new understanding of social relationships and social practices.

Processes as research focus

In applying an ethnographic approach, I found actual events in the fieldwork were different from what had been planned. I adapted to what happened, focused on these processes and transcended the boundaries of dualisms to enter social and educational processes. Out of these processes and settings, where events, social actors and discourses interacted with each other, I gathered data and findings. On this basis, research ideas and themes from a specific to a general level were extracted, categorized and interpreted.

Barriers created by dualisms in exploring international education and comparative education have been noted by researchers (e.g. McNess, Arthur and Crossley 2013; Robinson-Pant 2016). Take the dualism of insider/outsider for an example. 'We have moved into a new global intellectual context where research partnerships require insiders and outsiders to work together in new ways' (McNess, Arthur and Crossley 2013: 308). The outsider and the insider can be so shifting, fluid and slippery that they may go 'to a point where such distinctions become meaningless' (ibid, 310), and the insider/outsider distinction in ethnography 'pushes us to categorise and polarise peoples' identities, roles and knowledges' (Robinson-Pant 2016: 40).

Researchers have reconsidered this issue in different ways. McNess, Arthur and Crossley (2013) suggest the use of 'third space' on the basis of Bhabha's (1994) notion, encouraging 'intercultural dialogue, beyond the concepts of the insider and the outsider, that we can produce new meaning' that 'mut[u]ally enriches understanding' (McNess, Arthur and Crossley 2013: 312). Robinson-Pant (2016) starts by analysing the phenomenon of 'essentialising culture' in intercultural communication and argues that researchers turn away from the polarization of insider/outsider to 'develop greater understanding of the processes of comparative analysis' (53). This illuminates the idea that an ethnographic approach can be focused on the processes bridging insider/outsider polarizations to search for the meaning embedded.

On this basis, I expanded the insider/outsider dualism to such binaries as literate/illiterate, developer/developed, and researcher/researched to focus on processes. This enabled me to transcend the dualisms to examine reflexively changes, events and tensions within social and educational practices, and to conduct dialogues and interact with multiple actors, thus entering a world with no clear borders between the ideal world and the sensible world, which is, in Bogue's words, 'a curious interworld, in which bodies and words, things and ideas interpenetrate and the traditional demarcations between the physical and the metaphysical becomes blurred' (Bogue 1989: 54).

In this sense, my obsession, as noted at the beginning of this chapter, with a real, or physical, site, where I could conduct my fieldwork, could have been channelled into a virtual space, which could provide for a real yet a different form of research experiences. I thus contend that the most important factor for judging the success of an ethnographic research should not be determined by how well it has fulfilled its pre-designed research plans. Rather, it can be judged by the processes it captures, as these processes can transcend the dualisms, notably those between virtual and actual spaces, and develop further multiple processes. These processes contain both corporeal and incorporeal factors such as 'rules, resources, people, events and power' (Kabeer 1994), which interact and produce new processes, social relationships and identities.

Combining prior knowledge with theoretical lenses

As an ethnographer, I departed from my prior knowledge of migration history, adult learning and research methods such as participant observation, interviews, fieldnotes writing and data collection and analysis, as 'there is no escape from reliance on common-sense knowledge and methods of investigation' (Hammersley and Atkinson 2007: 18). In addition, I utilized ideas from such resources as the Deleuzian theories, the concept of development as discourse, and the approach of the Social Relations Framework (Kabeer 1994) as lenses, as Burgess (1984) argues that theoretical insights should be used to 'make seemingly irrational or paradoxical behaviour comprehensible' (79). In integrating various theories, I employed my reflexivity in negotiating between my prior knowledge and new knowledge, and amid co-functioning theories.

In exploring how the policies of the Yuanmeng plans transformed when encountering lower-level institutions and individuals, I noticed discrepant perceptions between education providers and learners towards these education projects. In the first few years of its practice, the Haibin Yuanmeng

Plan excluded local hukou student candidates from its courses. Over-emphasis of this education programme on migrant workers appeared to have harmed their sense of self-esteem. The Home of Migrants College insisted on using *nongmingong*, which literally means 'peasant workers', and was, as illustrated in Chapter 1, the earliest saying for 'rural migrant workers', all throughout its documents and even in the title of their college name.

Not every student in this college liked this label, as evidenced in my interview with Fang Xu, a student in the Home of Migrants College, to whom I taught English. Fang Xu was a volunteer for an amateur drama club while an administrator with a company for a living. On the weekends, there would be drama performances portraying migrant workers' life. I attended a drama show at Fang Xu's arrangement. Once she told me:

> I have hardly lived in the countryside. I came to Haibin with my parents when I was just a few years old. I have not got Haibin household register yet, so I am entitled nongmingong and have access to learning in the Home of Migrants College. But I hate being labelled with nongmingong.
> (Interview notes with Fang Xu, 18 May 2013)

Fang Xu was realizing her university dream with the Home of Migrants College; however, she felt offended by being labelled nongmingong. This contradiction prompted me to consider why those receiving assistance did not show gratitude to developers.

I thus encountered the concept of development as discourse, in which Escobar highlights the ways that local knowledge can be produced: 'the adaptation, subversions and resistance that local people effect in relation to development interventions' and 'the alternative strategies produced by social movements as they encounter development projects' (Escobar 2007: 21). The concept of development as discourse explains why there exist complexities residing in the contradictions between the developer and the developee, rather than a linear evolution course: assistance providing – achievements – and gratitude from beneficiaries. Some beneficiaries would return resentment for the offer. This concept offered me a lens through which to examine different and even conflicting responses towards education policies and practices from education providers and education receivers, and why there existed tensions and contradictions between different stakeholders in education projects.

However, my investigation process presented some revealing dimensions such as rules and resources. I attempted to explore why some rules were stipulated to recruit whom to access educational resources. The concept of development as discourse does not provide a convincing answer, as it tends to over-rely on the power of discourse, 'thus viewing the subject as a mere bearer and reproducer of a given discourse' (Lie 2008: 123). Consequently, I found problematic employing the concept of development as discourse, as this could neglect the power of other dimensions such as people and resources in transforming society and human subjectivities. Robinson-Pant (2016) maintains that, in applied education study, the multiple roles, social relationships and identities exerted by relevant stakeholders should be examined. This helped me turn away from overreliance on the approach of development as discourse and enter a zone of multiple perspectives and dimensions.

The approach of the Social Relations Framework (Kabeer 1994) was thus brought in to operationalize the concept of development as discourse. This approach analyses development policy and social relationships in terms of five interconnected dimensions: rules, activities, resources, people and power (1994: 281). It categorizes resources into human resources, tangible resources and intangible resources such as 'solidarity, contacts, information, political clout' (ibid, 280). However, it seemed to be problematic to clarify how these dimensions, as heterogenous elements, could be interlinked. The concept of assemblage developed by Deleuze and Guattari drives home how heterogeneous dimensions interact and interconnect. Deleuze and Guattari have explained the concept of assemblage in different contexts. For instance, Deleuze (1987), when being interviewed by Parnet, describes assemblage as:

> a multiplicity which is made up of many heterogeneous terms and which establishes liaisons, relations between them, across ages, sexes and reigns – different natures. Thus, the assemblage's only unity is that of co-functioning: it is a symbiosis, a 'sympathy'. It is never filiations which are important but alliances, alloys; these are not successions, lines of descent, but contagions, epidemics, the wind.
>
> (ibid, 69)

Deleuze and Guattari (1988: 7–9) further present five nomadic principles illustrating how heterogenous terms are mutually related: connection, heterogeneity, multiplicity, asignifying rupture and cartography and decalcomania. Some ideas could be summarized. Firstly, Deleuze and Guattari describe a plane where reside relations of heterogeneous entities. These relations interact with each other, producing further relations with other entities. In addition, the concept of assemblage is thought to embody features of fluidity, ephemerality, unpredictability and affective quality (Müller and Schurr 2016: 219). The connections between heterogenous entities are not always stable but can be fluid. This suggests that an assemblage is not a close ended area, but connected with other assemblages, within and among which an entity and connections of entities can be displaced. Thirdly, the concept of assemblage stresses 'the importance of the socio-material' and the idea that 'the world is made up of associations of human and non-human elements' (Müller and Schurr 2016: 217). Thus, the assemblage involves the role of affect, where desire is the vital force: 'desire only exists when assembled or machined. You cannot grasp or conceive of a desire outside a determinate assemblage, on a plane which is not pre-existent but which must itself be constructed' (Deleuze and Parnet 1987: 96).

In employing the concept of assemblage, I was aware that this concept suggesting fluidity, ephemerality and becoming could make analysis more elusive and non-focused. George E. Marcus and Erkan Saka (2006) advise those who wish to use this concept in ethnographic studies to take a moderate stance and focus on the attributes of heterogeneity and contingency: 'assemblage functions best as an evocation of emergence and heterogeneity amid the data of inquiry, in relation to other concepts and constructs without rigidifying into the thingness of final or stable states that besets the working terms of classic social theory' (106). Thereby, the concept of assemblage provided me with a lens to understand for how heterogeneous factors, such as resources and rules, were interconnected in the development of migrant workers' education.

In addition, this concept helped me explore how migrant workers' education as an assemblage was related to other assemblages. This understanding enabled me to connect the education study with a wider social context or its neighbouring areas. This resonates with the approach of the Social Relations

Framework, which suggests that the practice of development policy should be understood 'in a broader institutional context' (Kabeer 1994: 279). Thus, these two resources, as lenses for analysis, were brought into the area of migrant workers' education and subsequently extended into a wider scope of society. Accordingly, I did not restrict my analysis to the education programmes but pushed it into neighbouring zones of historical studies and migration studies. As a researcher, I was located on an assemblage where factors such as people, compassion and events were connected. This could offer an interpretation of my relationship with my research participants.

Drawing on the ideas from the approach of development as discourse, the approach of the Social Relations Framework and the concept of assemblage, I was able to focus on the dynamics of power relations within and across education institutions, explore how multiple and heterogeneous factors such as rules, resources and people were assembled and interlinked, and what results were produced from these processes.

Engaging the subjectivities of the researcher

In doing ethnography, I was reflecting on how I developed my understanding of this approach. As Hammersley and Atkinson (2007) claim, ethnography is generally concerned with 'developing theories' rather than 'testing existing hypothesis' (21). In this sense, as a link integrating virtualities and actualities, I generated and expanded ideas based on my fieldwork observations and my theoretical application.

I acted as both a researcher and a teacher, observing and contributing to curriculum practices in the Haibin Yuanmeng Plan. Meanwhile, I examined, mainly through online interview and data collection, the Yuanda Yuanmeng Plan targeted at migrant workers in a wider provincial scope. I was located at an 'interworld' (Bogue 1989: 54), where virtual spaces and actual spaces interconnected and interpenetrated. This enabled me to be actively engaged in certain educational and social processes, and even to plan and create events engaging research participants and bringing together different narrative voices. Thus, my research transcended the dualisms between virtual and actual spaces.

As mentioned above, in the ethnographic approach has emerged the transition from the pure objective observation, as suggested by Malinowski (1922) to the practice engaging the subjectivities of the ethnographer. This does not indicate complete change in the research methods such as participant observation and fieldwork notes taking. Rather, the radical change mainly resides in how to understand and interpret the observed data by engaging the subjectivities of the researcher, and on this basis, develop new findings.

3

Exploring Different Voices in Education Policies

As stated in Chapter 1, the state stresses the importance of adult learning for migrant workers. Two Yuanmeng plans have been in practice in Yuanda Province for over ten successive years. As government-sponsored education projects, the Yuanmeng plans shared many similarities. This chapter aims to present multiple voices on these education projects from policy makers, education practitioners and migrant workers as students in an attempt to understand the major concerns of policy makers, how policies were implemented, and the responses from migrant workers to adult-learning policies.

I will draw on the ideas from the concept of Deleuzian assemblage, the approach of the Social Relations Framework (Kabeer 1994) and the concept of development as discourse, as noted in Chapter 2. The purpose is to explore how education practices established assemblages, where heterogeneous factors such as discourses, social actors, educational resources, events and power connected and interacted, producing new relations and other factors.

Examining the focuses of education policies

As stated in Chapter 1, there were two education programmes for adult learning and migrant workers implemented in Yuanda Province: the Haibin Yuanmeng Plan and the Yuanda Yuanmeng Plan. Although having distinct full titles, the two education programmes were reduced to the same name 'the Yuanmeng Plan', which caused some confusion at times. This section compares these two programmes from the perspective of policy makers and education sponsors. It endeavours to track down the naming of these projects and its implications. In addition, it examines the rules for recruiting students and the discourses in curriculum design to identify the concerns in policy making.

Two Yuanmeng plans: Why the same name?

My spontaneous curiosity was why two different education programmes should have used the same name, which had caused confusion in Haibin City, where the Yuanda Yuanmeng Plan reached. To clarify, the Home of Migrants College issued a declaration in June 2012 on its official website: 'Serious declaration of Haibin General Trade Union "Yuanmeng Plan" Education Assistance Action for Needy Workers and nongmingong':

> Haibin General Trade Union 'Yuanmeng Plan' Education Assistance Action for Needy Workers and nongmingong was launched by Haibin General Trade Union and undertaken by the Home of Migrants College. The initiative began from May 2008 and has continued for five rounds...
>
> The 'Yuanmeng Plan' education assistance action has become a well-known brand in Haibin City and even in the circle of All China Trade Union...
>
> Recently, we have found that there is proceeding a similar initiative launched by other departments, which sounds the same as the 'Yuanmeng Plan' Education Assistance Action for Needy Workers and nongmingong in terms of naming, format and content. This has brought about confusion with our education action among general workers and nongmingong workers as well as in all walks of life.

The Home of Migrants College was not satisfied with the way Yuanmeng was claimed by another programme, which was the Yuanda Yuanmeng Plan, as would be confirmed with my gatekeeper after I started fieldwork in the Home of Migrants College.

The Home of Migrants College's response was understandable, as its education practice had been in progress for over four years since it began its education action in May 2008 and had won wide recognition. As the declaration claims, 'the "Yuanmeng Plan" is an original education public welfare brand with a complete intellectual property right possessed by the Haibin General

Trade Union'. Its contribution was remarkable. In the first five years from May 2008, according to the declaration,

> There are 150,000 nongmingong workers having received education and training of some sort supported by this education action. Concretely speaking, this project, according to the declaration, assisted 1094 students of model nongmingong in need of help to fulfill their university dreams, and supported 12,320 nongmingong in realising their dreams of vocational skills and 1,012 nongmingong in graduating from part time technical secondary school. We also offered public welfare 1,200 lectures to nongmingong and raised 26 million yuan over the five years.
> ('Serious declaration' of Haibin General Trade Union 2012)

Being a comprehensive programme, the Haibin Yuanmeng Plan offered academic degree courses, short-term vocational and technical training courses, and public lectures for an impressive number of learners. The announcement transmitted the college's sense of achievement.

What is interesting is that the Home of Migrants College had established an extensive social network in Haibin City and outside Yuanda Province. It provided lectures to different enterprises and social organizations, where migrant workers gathered, and acclaimed recognition from local and national media. In addition, high-rank officials from both central and local authorities 'showed their encouragement and support' 'by attending activities, participating in opening ceremonies and delivering important speeches' ('Serious declaration' of Haibin General Trade Union 2012).

Brief as this declaration was, '"Yuanmeng Plan" Education Assistance Action for Needy Workers and Nongmingong' was used eight times in its full title, showing that the Home of Migrants College was adamant about claiming 'the Yuanmeng Plan'.

Using the same name did cause some confusion, as evidenced by a series of online posts between Yuanmeng learners and the Home of Migrants College administrators:

> I have graduated from the Yuanmeng Plan for over a year. I am registered with Nanjing Diyi University. All the necessary procedures have been completed. But why couldn't I get a graduation certificate. This happened to all my classmates with this university...

> I have been in Haibin for three years. I want to pursue my university degree. I am 40 years old. I feel your age limit is inhuman. Aren't those older than 35 years humans? Can't we make contributions to our country?... I suggest that the Yuanmeng Plan should be open to all the Chinese people under 60 years old.
>
> (Fieldwork notes 17 October 2014)

Then followed by the official reply, 'based on the content of the complaints, these two students are not students of the Haibin Yuanmeng Plan sponsored by the Haibin General Trade Union. We have never made age limits, as we offer a lifelong education programme... We have never had partnerships with Nanjing Diyi University', and then warned the public against the 'fake brand Yuanmeng Plan': 'our partnership universities are not allowed to cooperate with other fake brand Yuanmeng plans'.

There was no way to track down why the Yuanda Yuanmeng Plan was so named at the turn of 2011 when the Haibin Yuanmeng had been in operation for three years or so. Strangely, the official title of the Yuanda Yuanmeng Plan had nothing of 'Yuanmeng' in it. As the Haibin Yuanmeng Plan was a municipal programme within Yuanda Province while the Yuanda Yuanmeng Plan a provincial one, the Haibin Yuanmeng Plan organizers had to be reconciled to the consequence, as admitted later in my interview with one of the staff in the Home of Migrants College.

To better understand the contested naming of the Yuanmeng plans, I attempt to link the naming of the Yuanmeng plans with the idea of Street (2011) on the naming of literacy. According to Street (2011), 'the power to define and name what counts as literacy and illiteracy also leads to the power to determine policy, to fund and develop literacy programmes in international contexts, to prescribe ways of teaching' (581). This suggests that the power to define and name 'literacy' is linked with a hierarchical relationship of power. In a similar vein, inequalities of power seemed to have surfaced from the naming of the Yuanmeng plans, at least from the perspective of the Home of Migrants College. However, if considered in the then Chinese social context, discourses around 'Yuanmeng' (dream fulfilment) had been overwhelming and represented in a wide range of contexts. Then there could be a different understanding for this naming practice: the programme designers of the Yuanda Yuanmeng Plan did not evidently plagiarize the naming, as illustrated in the following section.

Yuanmeng as a part of China's mainstream discourse

'Dream' (*meng* 梦) became a catch phrase from around 2012 onwards and was developed in every walk of life. 'The Chinese Dream' was elaborated on different occasions by China's president, Xi Jinping. Xi (2012) says: 'Now all of us are talking about the Chinese Dream. I think it is the greatest dream of the Chinese nation in modern times to realize the great rejuvenation of the Chinese nation'.

Later, on a different occasion, Xi (2013a) devoted a large space to the conception of the Chinese Dream in the words of grand narrative, like 'full union', 'national', 'common dream' and 'times'. Xi states: 'To realize the Chinese Dream, we must integrate all the forces in China. The Chinese Dream is a national dream and a dream for every Chinese person'. Soon afterwards, Xi (2013b) stressed the importance of labour in his speech, saying 'Beautiful dreams can be realized only through honest labour' before the International Labour day of 2013. According to him, 'all kinds of difficulties in the process of development can be resolved only through honest labour' (ibid), presenting such key words as 'beautiful', 'dream' and 'labour'.

One of the goals for the Yuanda Yuanmeng Plan was to 'develop an elite working force that the Communist Party of China can rely on'. This indicates that 'Yuanmeng' remained a part of the mainstream Chinese discourse. The Haibin Yuanmeng Plan responded closely to the discourse of Chinese Dream, as shown in a student recruitment advertisement of 2013:

> The sixth round of the Yuanmeng Plan, themed as 'The Chinese Dream and beautiful labour', is aimed at workers and migrant workers in meager family financial conditions as the objectives of assistance, offers free learning places of vocational training courses to 1000 workers and migrant workers, funds 1000 workers and migrant workers to fulfill their 'university dreams', and offers 500 public lectures themed as 'the Chinese Dream' to enterprises intending to enhance the workers' quality.
>
> (Fieldwork data, 06 June 2013)

Consequently, the discourses around university dream in the Haibin Yuanmeng Plan gained new legitimacy and momentum from 'the Chinese Dream', as they encouraged students to be well reconciled to professional labour. 'The university dream', thereby, became a constant discourse. This is an embodiment of intertextuality, which suggests that 'any text is the absorption and transformation of another' (Kristeva 1986: 37). From this perspective, the discourses around the university dream could be considered to have drawn on the then rising social ethos and social discourses calling for national rejuvenation. On this basis, these discourses were further enriched and developed by the discourses around the Chinese Dream.

However, whether the discourses around the university dream were accepted by the addressees depended on their prior knowledge, as 'a text's unity lies not in its origin but in its destination' (Barthes 1977: 148). With the increasing impact of the Chinese Dream and the publicity of the Yuanmeng Plan, migrant workers became acquainted with this programme and its themes through social connections and social media. They were thus actively engaged in developing the discourses around the university dream into various forms. For instance, I noticed a slogan of the Economic Management Class, who were admitted in the autumn of 2012, supervised by Beijing Skyline University, 'Coming for dreams and gathered because of miracle'. When I asked some students about their dreams in the Yuanmeng Plan, some told me in a formal way, and others smiled but offered no answers. The answers I received, in whatever way, all suggested: 'It is a university dream that we have not realized'.

The 'Yuanmeng' discourse had been integrated with the national discourse promoting a national dream while continuously developing into new directions such as the slogan of the Economic Management Class. Discourses, as Gee argues, 'split', 'meld' and change constantly, with new discourses appearing and old ones vanishing, 'defined in relationships of complicity and contestation with other Discourses', and existing in countless number (Gee 1999: 21–2). However, taking the concept of assemblage as a lens, the discourses can also be combined with other heterogeneous factors, sliding amid different assemblages with such factors as social connections, educational events, institutions, social actors and power. Likewise, the 'dream' discourses combined with and split from other discourses and factors, evolving into multiple forms. The university dreams of the students in the Home of Migrants College transformed into different states, including some undesirable malpractices. This will be further corroborated by the Haibin Yuanmeng Plan's curriculum practice in the next chapter on teaching practice.

The Yuanmeng plans as utilitarian projects

When discussing the relationship between the concept of development as a discourse and education planning and policy making, Robinson-Pant (2001) suggests that the focus could be on 'the political agendas of various development players' and 'the ideological dimension' (325). I have taken this idea to analyse the general design of the Yuanmeng plans, both of which prioritized ideological development in the process of practical learning.

The Yuanda Yuanmeng Plan prioritized the ideology of socialism but combined it with practical functions of education. It aimed to develop new generation industrial workers into a fundamental reliable force of the socialist country, complete 'an elite development project' to 'realize social management innovation among industrial workers', 'accelerate industrial upgrading', and 'establish the passageway of the new generation industrial workers' development and promotion' (the Yuanda Communist Youth League 2013). The Yuanda Provincial Government realized the inadequacy of labour-intensive manufacturing and the necessity to propel knowledge economy. It focused on how to enhance the human quality of a mass of 'elite' workers and acknowledged the importance of personal development of workers as learners.

A survey of the total curriculum of the Home of Migrants College in the Haibin Yuanmeng Plan presents a similar picture in that it attempted to consolidate socialist ideology combined with the instrumentality of adult learning. The total curriculum and its implications have been analysed in other countries. For instance, Kelly (2009) argues that the total curriculum of an educational institution is closely related to its whole education plan (9). I used this idea to explore implications of education policy embedded in the total curriculum of the Home of Migrants College. The total curriculum of this college comprehended aspects of life and professions: 'thought and politics, law, urban life, professional development, comprehensive quality, health, art of life, safe production and lifelong learning'. The first category of 'thought and politics' was closely connected with the major strands of China's ideology, as the college aimed to 'provide learners with the core values of socialism'. In addition, the total curriculum addressed how migrant workers could develop their skills and awareness to survive and serve urban society in such aspects as urban life, work and society. Based on this framework, a wide range of courses and subjects were provided for short-term vocational and technical training, long-term higher education academic courses, and public lectures. However, its focus was, like the Yuanda Yuanmeng Plan, on higher education courses.

The Yuanmeng plans were focused on academic degrees. This characteristic contradicted the findings of Zeng, Jia and He (2009), whose research was contextualized in the Pearl River Delta of China, show that over 80 per cent of their interviewees of migrant workers would prefer vocational training while only 16.7 per cent of them would choose degree courses. Thus, the Yuanmeng plans did not seem to have prioritized customising their teachings to the learners' needs.

In looking at the nature of the Yuanmeng plans, notably in terms of their policy design, teaching goals and contents, I have considered two contradictory perspectives: utilitarian and transformative. From the utilitarian perspective, the learning of knowledge and skills is closely connected with individual development and national economic and social development. Thus, education is 'a social investment' to ensure learners will become 'productive citizens within an established socio-economic order' (Maclure, Sabbah and Lavan 2012: 399). On the other hand, the transformative perspective sees education as an activity 'addressing the inequalities and injustices embedded in the larger society' (ibid, 400).

The Yuanmeng plans were designed for utilitarian purposes. Contextualized in socialist ideology, these programmes required learners to observe current social rules and practices and focused on the instrumentality of adult education in liberal marketing and rapid globalization; meanwhile, they encouraged personal development to be adapted to a commercialized society.

Student recruitment rules in the Yuanmeng plans

Rules were stipulated as to who were entitled to participate in the Yuanmeng plans. While the Yuanda Yuanmeng Plan focused on 'elite' workers, the Haibin Yuanmeng focused on 'needy' workers. This section will address what thoughts were embedded within the conditions and terms for recruiting students. The rules particularly interesting to me include age limits, *hukou* and whether good or poor students were to be selected. Some subtle differences in admission conditions existed between the Yuanda Yuanmeng Plan and the Haibin Yuanmeng Plan.

The age limit was specifically regulated in the Yuanda Yuanmeng Plan, which stated that course applicants must be 'above eighteen years old and below thirty-five'. For instance, the Yuanda Yuanmeng Plan for 2012 required that students be 'born between 1 July 1977 and 1 July 1994' (Lychee Municipal Government 2012). This was queried by some student candidates, such as the forty-year-old person, quoted above, 'So aren't those older than thirty-five years human beings?'

Discourse around age limits affected people's mentality and exercised effective control, as the ageism discourse seemed to have been naturalized in Chinese society. Examining job advertisements, which could be seen around industrial parks in Goods Town, Lychee City, would be telling. I saw an advertisement on the noticeboard of an electronic enterprise in November 2012 (see Figure 3.1). There have been changes in some respects such as income increase and working conditions in Goods Town in the recent years. However, I have decided to use this advertisement as a part of my historical account and discourse analysis, as I am mainly concerned about social implications embedded within this piece of writing, particularly in its requirements on age limits and learning backgrounds.

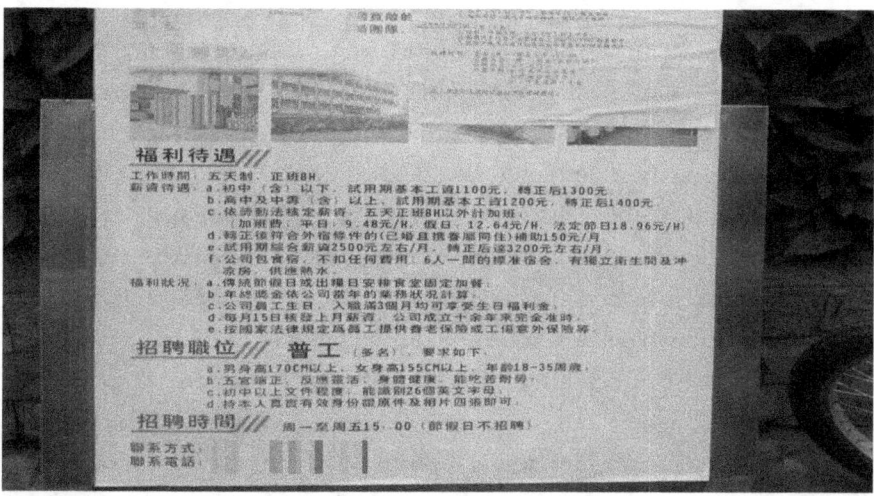

Figure 3.1 A job advertisement of an electronic factory in Goods Town, 2012. Taken by the author of this book

This advertisement, recruiting general workers, required that 'males to be no less than 170 cm and females no less than 155 cm with ages between 18 and 35 years old'. In addition to prejudiced height requirements, age limits were specified, which signalled that the older people were, the less worthy they were of being trained and employed.

This discursive strategy imposed mental control on migrant workers, notably the older ones, as shown below in my interview with Feng Jun, one of the security guards with a property management company in Lychee City. Feng Jun was an aspiring, industrious and practical man. He was concerned about current economic and social affairs. More than once, he mentioned proudly he was from the same place as Xi Jinping, the president of China. He was confident about the further development of his home province. Feng Jun was ready to leave this company for a factory. I expressed my wishes as a final goodbye:

'You are young, so you have many choices'.

Feng Jun grinned shyly: 'I am not young. I am over thirty-two years old now. You see many factories such as like Foxconn Group employ only people from eighteen to twenty-four years old. When you are older than that, you will not be employed. So, we are simply machines. We will be dumped when we are older and cannot work as fast as younger ones'.

(Fieldwork notes, 03 December 2012)

Although only thirty-two years old, Feng Jun no longer thought of himself young. The internal anxiety around aging could be perceived in his tone. Kabeer (1994) points out the impact of rules: when immersed in an institution, the rules could be taken as 'natural or immutable' (282). Similarly, the impact of ageism discourses in recruiting workers and students upon migrant workers could be identified, as they had been perpetuated in the rapidly industrialized society. However, hardly anyone in my fieldwork raised queries about the soundness and mutability of these social rules and conventions. Discourses around ageing and their negative impact have also been noted in the international context. For instance, Lytle and Levy (2019) point out that older adults tend to be represented as negative and face discrimination in everyday life and employment. Thus, they explored how to apply ageism reduction intervention programmes to combat ageism. To reduce discourses around ageing and their negative impact, UNESCO's (2020) report on the future of lifelong learning recommends adopting an appropriate pedagogical approach 'that contributes to a more positive representation of ageing' (8).

Hukou (household registration) was the second condition for the Yuanmeng plans. The Haibin Yuanmeng Plan required that only non-Haibin rural household register holders be allowed to take the Yuanmeng academic courses. Those who were of the Haibin household register but wanted to take these courses should be confirmed as grassroots Trade Union cadres, as confirmed Zheng Zhiyong, a student of the Haibin Yuanmeng Plan, in his class QQ chat room: 'I could not join this programme if I should apply for it now, as I have now a Haibin household register' (QQ chat record, 03 May 2013). The Haibin Yuanmeng Plan upheld its initial principle of assisting the 'real' migrant workers. This excluded local workers from educational resources.[1]

By contrast, the Yuanda Yuanmeng Plan did not impose restrictions on its student recruitment based on the household register, on condition that they had been employed with a local enterprise for a year. Many other places in Yuanda Province, such as Lychee City, referred to migrant workers as wailaigong (外来工), which meant workers from outside, as stated in Chapter 1. This change in definition was reflected in the titling of the Yuanda Yuanmeng Plan, which stressed 'new generation leading workers' as the target of its working plan. This implies that the Yuanda Yuanmeng Plan included not only local but also outside workers; it did not differentiate between rural and urban migrant workers. The Yuanda Yuanmeng Plan was more inclusive in terms of household register types.

The third condition for the Yuanmeng plans was the assessment of students' literacy levels and learning abilities. The Haibin Yuanmeng Plan was concerned about 'the needy workers'. It was more comprehensive in its educational courses, including both academic programmes for elite workers and short-term courses such as property management, tea making art and flower arrangement art. The Yuanda Yuanmeng Plan required that student candidates possess senior middle school qualifications to be admitted to academic degree courses. In other words, migrant workers, such as Zhang Xiaohu and his workmates in the property management company, were not considered to be educated enough for this programme.

One of the first interviews with Zhang Xiaohu was conducted around seven o'clock evening time. It was still bright at this time of the year in southern China with the setting sun glowing. Zhang Xiaohu invited me to go into their stand, also their office, where I could sit leisurely with air conditioning on. It was hot and humid outside. There were two guards, one watching the gate for half an hour and the other staying inside the stand. He said sighing:

> I did not do well at school. I only finished the first year of my junior middle school and then quitted. When I was a student, I was absent-minded in class time. I could not help it. I was naughty. Then I came to Lychee City over ten years ago.
>
> (Interview notes, 18 October 2012)

Zhang Xiaohu, in his early thirties, came from a rural area in Shaanxi Province, west China. He fell in love with a colleague, from Hubei Province, central China. They had been married for a few years with two children, left to his parents back at Shaanxi Province. Although working in factories for a few years, Zhang Xiaohu could not stand noisy environment and working conditions, or in his words, he could not 'suffer'. Thus, in most of the years, he worked as a security guard for property management. He seemed to relate his living status and conditions with his low literacy performance. Zhang Xiaohu was not an exception in terms of having a poor educational background and low literacy levels. I interviewed some other migrant workers in Goods Town, Lychee City, but none of them had learned of the Yuanda Yuanmeng Plan. Thus, this plan was not meant for Zhang Xiaohu and his like, as they were not considered to be 'good' enough to be 'elite' students.

I have discussed the general policies of the Yuanda Yuanmeng Plan and the Haibin Yuanmeng Plan. The Yuanda Yuanmeng Plan focused on 'elite' workers by providing them with academic degree programmes to transform and upgrade the industry of Yuanda Province. Its purpose was to bring in more creative vigour into its industrial sector. The Haibin Yuanmeng Plan focused on 'needy' workers and pushed programmes both academic and technical and vocational, thus being more inclusive of learners of different levels and needs.

Although the goal of the Yuanda Yuanmeng Plan was to develop new generation industrial workers into an elite working force, this was intended to be for 'younger' people within certain age groups. Likewise, though the goal of the Haibin Yuanmeng Plan was focused on 'the needy' workers, it excluded the workers with Haibin local household registers who could be considered as more 'needy' for education and training. The rules for recruiting students influenced the mentality of student candidates for the Yuanmeng plans, triggering their anxiety over issues such as ages, identities and low-educational qualifications.

The rules for recruiting students suggest that the Yuanmeng plans excluded some groups of students in terms of age limits, literacy levels and household register types. As these rules tended to conceal prejudice against certain groups of people under the guise of drawing on the discourses of 'needy' and 'elite', they seemed to have been normalized by programme practitioners and migrant workers.

What is noteworthy, there arose queries from migrant workers on the legitimacy of these rules, indicating their awakening new subjectivities. As discussed above, some workers voiced their queries around the rules for admission to the Yuanmeng plans. When workers accumulated discontent, they started to challenge the normalized discourses, thus breaking with the established discursive order and gaining new subjectivities, or in the words of Deleuze and Guattari, making 'asignifying rupture' (1988: 9) from the current assemblage, where they were located, and slid and floated onto a new plane.

Examining the concerns of education practitioners

This section addresses how education practitioners reacted to the Yuanmeng plans, especially how they gained access to tangible resources such as funding resources and intangible resources such as social contacts and networks, to survive in a competitive education market. I am concerned to explore how far the heterogeneous connections between factors, notably power, rules and resources, were made, which, in turn, produced other factors, for example new resources and educational activities.

Funding resources and disbursement

Both the Yuanmeng plans had been allocated funding resources to support their education design and implement their educational activities, but they had different funding sources. The Haibin Yuanmeng Plan relied on the Haibin General Trade Union while the Yuanda Yuanmeng Plan relied on governmental departments of different levels as its major funders and some other social organizations and enterprises, thus reflecting more complicated social relations.

In the Home of Migrants College, as mentioned in the declaration cited above, '26 million yuan' (around 2.6 million pounds) was disbursed from 2008 to 2012. As the funding amount varied from year to year, I was curious about who funded this programme. Wang Shaogang, Vice President of the Home of Migrants College, replied succinctly, 'It is the Haibin General Trade Union, as they have collected membership fees, of course they should support workers' education'. (Interview notes with Wang Shaogang, 21 October 2012)

I was also interested in some details of the funding, such as the amount of funding and the number of the students recruited, as well as any concrete requirements for the evaluation of students' vocational training courses. Xiao Zhiyuan, my gatekeeper, shared with me his knowledge about it:

> We have no competitors in the Yuanmeng Plan funding and actually we perform the roles of the Haibin General Trade Union, as our college is its subordinate and the only designated institution for the implementation of the Yuanmeng Plan. Every year in March, we would report relevant working and budgeting plans for this programme to the Haibin General Trade Union. Then the General Trade Union allots half of the fund and the rest of it will be disbursed by the end of year according as how much we have completed our work... Overall, our funding has been on the increase from 2008 onwards.
> (QQ interview with Xiao Zhiyuan, 05 March 2013)

It seems that there had been sufficient funding for the Haibin Yuanmeng Plan, and the General Trade Union offered full support for this programme. This ensured the consistency and sustainability of this education project over a considerable period. In addition, in contrast with other educational institutions in the Yuanda Yuanmeng Plan, the Home of Migrants College acted for the

Haibin Trade Union, as it was the only authorized educational institution. This guaranteed its power and advantages in policy design, partnerships and educational practice.

By contrast, the Yuanda Yuanmeng Plan involved more funding sources. To raise funding, Yuanda provincial government mobilized different levels of authorities and enterprises including those in Haibin City. As stated in Chapter 1, the Lychee City 2012 Action Plan for the Yuanda Yuanmeng Plan shows that Lychee Waterfront University was nominated as the only educational partner for that year.

> After negotiating between the Yuanmeng Office of Lychee City and Lychee Waterfront University, the latter agrees to deduct 500 yuan on the basis of the 5000 yuan stipulated by Yuanda Province. As a result, the tuition fee for every student is now 4,500 yuan, among which each student pays 1000 yuan, with 2000 yuan financed by Yuanda provincial authorities, and 1500 yuan financed by Lychee municipal and township authorities.
> (Lychee Municipal Government 2012)

This shows there were complex negotiations among multiple stakeholders. Funding sources mainly came from different levels of authorities. However, Lychee Waterfront University, as a contractor of this programme, was willing to offer concessions as it had won an important opportunity to expand its educational spaces against other competitive rivals. Thus, there happened a discontinuity in the educational practice of the Yuanda Yuanmeng in Lychee, or an 'asignifying rupture' (Deleuze and Guattari 1988: 9), as it broke with Beijing Lakeview University in the 2012 academic year. There was a compromise and transaction between the local municipal government and Lychee Waterfront University, as a local institution. They excluded Beijing Lakeview University as an external institution from their assemblage of resources and activities, though this university was the pioneering partnership institution in Lychee for the Yuanda Yuanmeng Plan.

The changes in educational partnerships in Lychee reflect changing power relations, spawning rather limited choices for students in education access. Some student candidates for this programme queried this arrangement, as will be discussed in the next section.

It appeared that sufficient funding ensured a constant influx of students and smooth progress of education courses each year. Funding as a dynamic force propelled the education projects within interconnected and interpenetrating webs of relationships. The Haibin Yuanmeng Plan and the Yuanda Yuanmeng Plan assumed distinct patterns in allocating resources. The funding appealed to educational institutions and agents. Correspondingly, diverse activities to recruit students were launched to acquire funding.

Recruiting students through a campaign

It remained a consistent task for educational institutions and agencies to recruit eligible students for the Yuanmeng plans. This was reliant on social networks and collaboration.

In the Yuanda Yuanmeng Plan, recruiting students involved a large-scale campaign, in which myriad institutions, agencies and social actors participated. For instance, Lychee Seabreeze Academy, as introduced in Chapter 1, was involved in the Yuanda Yuanmeng Plan in 2011. As an educational agency, it coordinated a few educational institutions offering Yuanmeng distance courses and supported their teaching affairs and student recruitment.

Another example is how Beijing Lakeview University changed its strategies in the Yuanda Yuanmeng Plan. As the only pioneering institution for this programme and one of the top universities in China, Beijing Lakeview University set an example in early 2011 by offering academic courses to 100 students for the first year Yuanda Yuanmeng. From then on, the discourse landmark of 'Yuanmeng 100' was created. However, as more educational institutions joined this programme, Beijing Lakeview University seemed to have realized it was losing power to other rivals. So, in the 2014 Yuanda Yuanmeng Plan, it strengthened its student recruitment campaign. It employed agencies across Yuanda Province to recruit students. One of its agents even called on the students in one of my QQ chat rooms to forward their advertisement to new student candidates.

Likewise, in the Home of Migrants College in the Haibin Yuanmeng Plan, recruiting students was a task for the staff each year. At the beginning, it only admitted students once a year but later they did it twice a year. What is more, student candidates could sit entrance exams for an unlimited number of times until they passed them but paid only once for the successful attempt. To encourage current registered students to advertise and promote its Yuanmeng courses, the Home of Migrants College put forward an incentive plan in 2013: anyone who successfully recommended a student to be admitted to a Yuanmeng academic degree course would be offered a second chance to take a higher degree Yuanmeng academic course. This was no different from a commercialized promotional strategy. Even Zhao Daming, the tutor of the Economic Management Class, as introduced in Chapter 1, called on his students in his class QQ chat room: 'The recruitment task for Yuanmeng 2013 is approaching the final stage. Hope everyone here will be a volunteering promoter, letting known this good news to your friends around' (QQ chat record, 30 May 2013).

In addition, the staff from the college head to the general clerks in the Home of Migrants College participated in student recruitment campaign, according to the college report in May 2013. They 'went down to over 100 enterprises' to disseminate the Haibin Yuanmeng Plan and encourage migrant workers to be engaged. They publicized this education programme by 'various means such as newspapers, banners, pamphlets, TV media and the internet'. The report ended by saying: 'We believe that, with our joint effort, we will fulfill the task of student recruitment this year' (the Home of Migrants College report 2013).

Clearly, recruiting students was taken as an important assignment by the college, which was closely connected with how much funding would be allocated from the authorities, thus guaranteeing the development of the college.

Recruitment of students was followed by entrance exams in diverse ways. This enabled admission procedures to be flexible. The Haibin Yuanmeng had relatively stable and consistent methods of entrance exams, which were multiply offered all throughout the year.

However, in the Yuanda Yuanmeng Plan, different sets of entrance exams were adopted, as there were many educational institutions in a sprawling pattern. Generally, each distance-learning institution administered its own entrance exams. However, in the practice of Lychee City in 2012, things changed. As the only Yuanda Yuanmeng Plan contractor and a local university in Lychee City, Lychee Waterfront University did not have the right to offer distance-learning courses; it could not offer entrance exams to student candidates on its own. As a result, it had to recruit students through China national adult higher education exams (Lychee Municipal Government 2012).

To acquire funding, educational institutions, agencies and actors were devoted to recruiting students. Ways of recruiting student were diverse, involving complex relations at different levels. Along with recruitment campaigns, students' admissions assumed multiple and flexible forms, distinct from traditional full time higher education entrance examinations. The diversity of recruitment and admission processes meant that student candidates could have more chance of accessing the Yuanmeng plans. This also indicated that disparate entrance standards could be adopted; consequently, entrance quality would be difficult to monitor and assess.

I have discussed the concerns and practices of education practitioners in terms of funding resources and their allocation, and student recruitment and admission. There emerged a clear commercialization process involving governmental investment and social participation through the Yuanmeng plans.

Analysis shows that there existed complex relations in funding resources and relevant activities. As heterogeneous factors, student recruitment campaigns were combined with resources such as funding and social relations, which, in turn, produced closer educational partnerships as intangible resources and maintained the workings of educational institutions.

Educational institutions and commercial agencies in the Yuanmeng plans were involved in a complicated competition for financial support. In this process, the government appeared to have set up this competition between educational institutions and commercial agencies. To reach this aim, social relationships were formulated and reshuffled. Activities such as student recruitment campaigns and flexible admissions were launched and implemented.

Examining the responses of learners

The Yuanmeng plans, as top-down education initiatives, were mainly negotiated between institutions and authorities. In this process, students largely remained the absent 'other'. This section addresses what migrant workers as learners thought about adult learning, especially the education programmes for migrant workers.

'Only excellent employees are recommended'

Having discussed how education providers launched campaigns to recruit students in the Haibin Yuanmeng Plan, I was interested in how students were admitted to their courses, and found that at the grassroots level of adult education, there existed a close relationship between workers and the branches of the Haibin General Trade Union in distributing educational resources.

After an English session for the Economic Management Class in the Home of Migrants College, I had an interesting discussion with a few students from a bus company, where they acted as ticket conductors. When I asked who could be Yuanmeng students in their company, Lingling, a dynamic girl, replied without any hesitation, 'In our company, only excellent employees are recommended. When we are graduated, we can get 1000 yuan as bonus' (interview notes, 17 March 2013). I could see Lingling's eyes sparkling with sense of pride, as she had been recommended and admitted to the current course. Her determined response indicated that such discourse 'excellent employees' was a criterion for the Yuanmeng students from their company. When I further asked about the meaning of 'excellent employees', Meili, one of my key informants in the Haibin Yuanmeng Plan, replied succinctly, 'abiding by company rules, without record of breaking company disciplines' (interview notes, 17 March 2013). Lingling and Meili appeared to have taken this rule, which had been perpetuated within their company, as 'natural or immutable' (Kabeer 1994: 282).

As revealed in its title, the Haibin General Trade Union 'Yuanmeng Plan' Education Assistance Action for Needy Workers and Nongmingong was to assist the 'needy' workers who needed learning support. However, when implemented, the bus company was more concerned if student candidates were 'excellent' employees. It seemed that the discourse in policy design seemed to have experienced some transformations in the stage of education practice. These transformations could be seen as the results via 'adaptation, subversions and resistance' and 'the alternative strategies' (Escobar 2007: 21) when developmental interventions came down to local enterprises.

There existed deep structures of power dynamics in recommendation of students for learning opportunities. Kabeer asserts that power over people can be constructed 'through its norms, its distribution of resources and responsibilities and its practice' (Kabeer 1994: 282). This understanding can be taken to analyse the power relations in the Haibin Yuanmeng Plan embedded in its use of educational rules, resources and activities. As the company did not focus on the 'needy', but on the 'excellent', it would be up to the company officials to decide who would be recommended for education opportunities. Thus, the company was to impose compliance on its own staff. It used ambiguous words like 'excellent', a disguised version for 'obedient', to conceal its desire to control its staff.

However, some migrant workers as students were not necessarily always 'obedient'. They uttered their different opinions to change the route towards education projects co-designed by policy makers and practitioners, as discussed below.

'Only a local institution nominated as an educational partner'

Lychee Waterfront University was nominated as the sole education provider in 2012–2013 academic year for Lychee City in the Yuanda Yuanmeng Plan. As mentioned earlier in this chapter, there was some controversy shown in the QQ chat room. Official reports did not specify why Lychee Waterfront University was so designated. Lychee City had delayed official student admission again and again until April 2013. In addition, prospective students in Lychee City would have to take national entrance exams for adult higher education, as Lychee Waterfront University was not qualified to offer online distance-learning courses but only correspondence courses with regular face-to-face instruction throughout the academic year.

Some students were not satisfied with this arrangement. There arose a heated discussion on this issue in a Yuanda Yuanmeng QQ chat room. Chuan Aixiang expressed his opinions. Chuan Aixiang was then a student of the Yuanda Yuanmeng Plan and a technician with a Japanese-invested electronic product company stationed in Haibin City. We have been in close contact since then.

> Chuan Aixiang: It is not nice that Yuanda is practising local protectionism.
> Mingming: Agree.
> Chuan Aixiang: At the beginning, Beijing Lakeview University was the only institution for this programme, but later some institutions lower on the ranking list joined in. But now, only the local one.

Fei Xiang: This is so-called the pattern of trial, copy and then promotion.
(QQ chat record, 30 May 2013)

Fei Xiang's 'trial, copy and then promotion' was from the initial slogan of the Yuanda Yuanmeng Plan, which expected Beijing Lakeview University to be a role model for other partner institutions. Obviously, Fei Xiang was being sarcastic.

In the implementation of the Yuanmeng plans, QQ online chatrooms connected policy makers and education practitioners either directly or indirectly. It was hard to determine whether students' discussions made a difference to the policy changing. But Lychee City changed its practice one year later. Lychee Waterfront University acted as the only institution for the Yuanda Yuanmeng Plan for just one year. In the latter half of 2013, Lychee City added two more partners: Lychee Technical College and Zhejiang Evergreen University from Zhejiang Province.

Constant adjustments in partnership institutions indicate that there had been a negotiation between different parties. The main consideration seemed to be to retain Lychee Waterfront University, and later Lychee Technical College, which were two local institutions, to strengthen local relationships. In the latter half of 2013, statistics show that Lychee Waterfront University recruited 1,400 students and Lychee Technical College recruited 400 students, but Zhejiang Evergreen University, a key university in China, recruited only 200.

The cooperation between Lychee local authorities and local educational institutions could be compared to the research study of Lebeau and Bennion (2014) conducted in the different context of the UK. They argue that universities contributed to local development depending on 'their position on the higher education market as much as by their embeddedness in the local economy, culture and polity' (278). Similarly, Lychee Waterfront University, though not provincially influential, was supported financially by local authorities and experienced more embeddedness in local socio-economic development, thus strengthening competitiveness in the China's higher education market.

There proceeded some negotiation between institutions in distributing resources such as funding and education opportunities. As everybody is caught in relations of power, the students were involved in a relationship involving government, enterprises and educational institutions. Along with their increasing power, they played a part in changing the layout of the Yuanmeng education and its development patterns. This was all the clearer when modern technological communication devices such as QQ messengers helped establish a platform for migrant workers as students. This platform could be seen as an 'interworld' where 'bodies, and words, things and ideas interpenetrate' (Bogue 1989: 54), and where their voices were instantaneously spread and heard by other social actors and institutions, thus contributing to changes in education practices.

Social relations as an important means to accessing learning opportunities

When examining adult learners' access to educational opportunities, I found different degrees in utilizing social relations to access learning opportunities like the Yuanmeng plans.

There were various forms of social connections for migrant workers: governmental organizations, educational institutions, enterprises, social associations and virtual space associations. The Haibin Yuanmeng Plan saw an increasing leverage of the Haibin General Trade Union, as it appeared on many occasions and public media such as websites and promotion brochures. Likewise, the Yuanda Communism Youth League was also spreading its influence across the whole province. Thus, migrant workers would have access to learning opportunities if they were in close relation to the branches of governmental organizations or worked with enterprises of good social publicity.

The interview notes with Meili, one of my key informants and a coordinator from a bus company in Haibin City, show that there were different channels through which to acquire information for the Haibin Yuanmeng Plan and certain criteria by which to be admitted to this programme. Meili acquired the Haibin Yuanmeng information from a website but some of her classmates from the same company saw its advertisement in their own company or advised by office workers (interview notes with Meili, 10 April 2013).

It appears that well-informed migrant workers on good terms with their employers were provided with more chances for personal promotion and further education. This can be linked with Cheung and Wu's (2011) research in the context of Chinese business management, which demonstrated that good personal relationship between supervisors and subordinates could enable subordinates to 'gain access to valuable information, power, and referrals from their supervisor' (359). Similarly, Meili's colleagues received support and referrals from their supervisors for learning resources.

What is more, migrant workers as students in the Haibin Yuanmeng Plan tended to be concentrated in some large-scale companies such as the bus company cited above, where the Trade Union was active and dynamic, with its sub-branches stationed. So not surprisingly, there were more students registered with the Yuanmeng plans from some enterprises than from others, because in the former there existed a well-organized system of information and contact. Also, those with close personal contact with relevant departments had more access to educational interventions. This point could be related to the idea of Kabeer that the value of social relations are intangible resources, through which the 'most productive activities' can be 'carried out' (1994: 280).

However, those who worked with a small enterprise or a factory seldom knew of further education opportunities sponsored by governments or social organizations. This was shown from my observation of security guards from the property management company, where Zhang Xiaohu and Feng Jun, as mentioned earlier in this chapter, worked:

> I asked Zhang Xiaohu: 'Did you take any training?'
> 'No', he said, 'it is too expensive, and needs a lot of time. I want to do some business. If only I could learn skills of management. But I think this sort of thing can be learned well in practice rather than in school. A few years ago, when insurance business was popular, I had wanted to take some courses about it. But it was time consuming and costly'.
> His partner, a young man in his early twenties, a new face, replied, 'Sometimes, you do not have to pay. Sometimes, they train you'. He occasionally joined our conversation while watching the gate in case cars were driving in or out so that he would lift the bar or put it down and let cars leave or come in.
> I asked them if they knew of Yuanmeng plans, both replied: 'No, I have never heard of this'.
>
> (Fieldwork notes 04 November 2012)

This new young man had joined this company recently and used to work with a hotel, as a security guard as well, in Haibin City. Zhang Xiaohu had remained in a secluded circle while his workmate had working experiences in a big hotel, thus had different social knowledge from Zhang Xiaohu. In addition, he did not have enough free time to establish wide social connections, as he had to work many shifts due to inadequate material conditions, as shown below:

> While interviewing Zhang Xiaohu and his workmate, a middle-aged man came to the gate, asking: 'Are you still recruiting security guards?' Zhang Xiaohu and his partner said warm-heartedly: 'Yes, we are'. The man asked how much money he could make. Zhang Xiaohu replied: '2000 yuan a month for the first month and then 2100 yuan from the second month on, 300 yuan subsidiary offered for meals, accommodation given and three days' break each month. Each day working 12 hours'.
>
> (Fieldwork notes on 18 October 2012)

This middle-aged man was known as Lao Yang and later became one of my key informants. Zhang Xiaohu quoted uninterruptedly working conditions, suggesting his familiarity with company rules. The stories of Zhang Xiaohu and his colleagues can be explored through Kabeer's (1994: 280) contention on the significance of social relations as an important means by which to produce further intangible resources, strengthen material foundations and implement activities. Zhang Xiaohu and his colleagues worked twelve hours each day with only three days' break each month; this did not provide him with enough time or energy to nurture efficient social relations as intangible resources. Not surprisingly, they had no access to productive activities such as education programmes focused on migrant workers.

Therefore, such places as those where Zhang Xiaohu worked needed more education interventions. There existed a vast disparity between those with efficient social connections and those without them. This showed that it was not enough for government to allocate resources to educational sector but there was a need to ensure that the resources would be reasonably distributed and harnessed. The education policies underwent transformations in the top-down process of implementation, and educational partners could use their power over migrant workers in distributing educational resources.

Acquiring funding support for learning

The Yuanmeng plans, as discussed earlier in this chapter, disbursed funding for migrant students from the authorities of different levels. Educational institutions competed for the funding through different channels. In a similar vein, migrant workers needed to obtain funding support to fulfil adult formal learning. This section explores how material conditions impacted the learning of migrant workers.

The section above shows that migrant workers, such as Zhang Xiaohu, did not possess adequate material conditions for educational opportunities. To survive, they worked twelve hours each day with three days' break for each month. Thus, they were unable to escape from this assemblage where they did long shifts with limited social connections and inadequate income. To protect the wellbeing of migrant workers, the government stipulated relevant regulations, notably the rule on minimum income. However, some enterprises took countermeasures when processing workers' request for augmenting income. As Lao Yang, mentioned above, who had joined the property management team, complained:

> The team leader was rather undemocratic. Some of us asked that they should have their monthly salary increased according to the government announcement. He said: 'OK', and then he cut off the original bonus and allowance, and put it in the salary package, saying: 'This is the minimum salary'. Then there remained the same without any changes. Two old colleagues wanted to resign after their probation period, which was actually a threat, as they did not really want to leave. The team leader said: 'OK, but you just have the salary at 2,000 yuan designated before the probation. If you want to go, I will sign for your resignation'. You know they are old. Hard to find a new job. Actually, the team leader did not want to keep them. He saved 100 yuan from each person, but he should have paid them 2.100 yuan instead.
>
> (Interview notes with Lao Yang, 06 May 2013)

Lao Yang's remark shows inconsistent practices existed in implementing salary terms with some organizations or enterprises. By 'undemocratic', Lao Yang was suggesting 'not willing to compromise'. The use of this formal political term indicates that Lao Yang had certain sense of his own right as an employee and a citizen. At the same time, government's salary policies encouraged the security guards to negotiate with the management for their own welfare. But it turned out to be difficult, as there seemed to be no effective supervisory mechanism but just some governmental guidance.

To avoid disputes over payment, some companies put forward clear items on working hours and amount of payment, as detailed in the job advertisement of Figure 3.1:

> Working time: five days per week, eight hours each day;
>
> Salary and allowances:
>
> a. Those who have had junior middle school education or below are paid a monthly salary of 1,100 yuan on probation while 1,300 yuan afterwards;
> b. Those who have had senior middle school or technical vocational school education or above are paid 1,200 on probation and 1,400 when permanently employed;
> c. Salary to be calculated according to labour law: aside from eight hours per day; five days per week, 9.48 yuan per hour is paid for weekdays, 12.64 per hour for holidays, and 18.96 yuan per hour for festivals;
> d. Those who are permanently employed and qualified to be accommodated outside (married with dependent families), 150 yuan per month is provided;
> e. For those on probation, the total income per month is 2,500 yuan while 3,200 yuan for those permanently employed.

A gap was perceived between the stipulated working time and the actual working time. The advertisement claimed 'five days per week, eight hours each day'; however, this schedule would bring a monthly income less than 1,400 yuan. Thus, workers were expected to do extra shifts to make more money, at least, to reach a figure over 2,500 yuan.

Thereby, around Mountainview Village, working at nighttime for extra hours was common for migrant workers so that I could see lights here and there from the factories, along with noises from machines or working tools. The government issued rules such as stipulating minimum wages to support workers, but supervision seemed to be ineffective. Thus, enterprises such as the property management ignored these rules or randomly interpreted them.

Most migrant workers did not seem to possess enough time, or material conditions, to participate in education programmes such as the Yuanmeng plans. In addition, restrictions of literacy levels excluded quite a percentage of migrant workers from the learning opportunities, as the Yuanda Yuanmeng Plan, as discussed above, was focused on elite students to develop an elite working force. Consequently, funding and learning resources were allocated to those with better upward mobility, as exemplified in the experiences of Chuan Aixiang, a beneficiary of the Yuanda Yuanmeng Plan.

As mentioned above, Chuan Aixiang, a student of the Yuanda Yuanmeng Plan, was one of the key informants for the Yuanda Yuanmeng Plan. He told me more than once: 'If there had not been funding for taking this degree course, I might not have taken it'. Chuan Aixiang never told me about his monthly income. When I tried to guess an amount at 4,000 yuan, he told me 'more than that'. This was understandable as Chuan Aixiang was a student towards a bachelor's degree, better educated than many other migrant workers as learners. Then tuition fees of around 5,000 yuan or so for the Yuanda Yuanmeng Plan, as discussed earlier in this chapter, would not be a big problem for him even if he had to pay on his own. However, things were not that seemingly simple. If Chuan Aixiang had not been registered as a student in the Yuanda Yuanmeng Plan but wished to do a degree course with an educational institution, then he would have paid over 10,000 yuan. That would be a considerable sum.

Therefore, there seemed to be a transaction between the Yuanda Yuanmeng Plan and participating partnership institutions: as this education project recruited a large number of students, educational institutions and agencies would charge students half the original price. Thus, learners in the Yuanda Yuanmeng Plan received an offer from a promotion activity, similar to any other commercial promotion. From the perspective of funding as a tangible resource, the above discussion shows the importance of funding for individual learners in the Yuanmeng plans. Acquiring funding support for the learners was a result of the negotiation between authorities, enterprises and educational institutions.

Migrant workers, such as Zhang Xiaohu and his workmates, working and living around Goods Town, Lychee City, seemed to be on totally different assemblages from the Yuanmeng students. Unlike the Yuanmeng students, many migrant workers in Goods Town did not seem to access efficient social networks, sufficient funding or educational resources in relation to these formal learning programmes. This brought my attention to an increasing stratification of migrant workers. To access educational programmes such as the Yuanmeng plans, migrant workers would need to gain some conditions – enough free time, adequate income, social connections and funding support. Meanwhile, the educational opportunities were likely to increase the gap between migrant workers in social and educational status and contribute to their own stratification.

Tensions in education policies and their implementation

By adopting multiple perspectives, I examined issues concerning the Yuanmeng plans and explored the discourses, performances and perceptions from policy makers, education providers, enterprises and migrant workers. I found embedded tensions in these education policies and practices, showing the changing discourses and social relationships.

Rules as institutionalized discourse appeared to have a strong influence on people. Some migrant workers were aware that some rules were not solidly based. When immersed in these discourses, people would have normalized them. However, different views were uttered by some students, as mentioned in their queries towards the Home of Migrants College and their challenging comments on Lychee Waterfront University as being designated as the only education provider in Lychee City. This suggests that discourses and power were not fixed or static but flowing and transforming. Some migrant workers were able to deviate from the institutionalized rules, thus raising their concerns and contributing to the changing of education policy and practice. This can be supported by Kabeer's (1994) idea that in a development project, there could be 'a bottom-up back flow of evaluative information into the planning process' (302).

For instance, the Haibin Yuanmeng Plan imposed restrictions on Haibin local hukou holders but was mainly opened to migrant workers with non-Haibin rural hukou, thus over-emphasizing the identity of migrant workers but excluding local workers. However, moving forward, I found that its student recruitment guidelines for 2020 have become more inclusive, putting workers with Haibin local hukou at the top of the list. Policy makers seemed to have adjusted their plans to the feedback from the grassroots level.

In addition, there emerged some changes in discourses concerning personal development and national needs in comparison with the times before the reform and opening. The Yuanmeng plans reflected mainly the intentions of the funders and organizers. Collective and national interests were emphasized by policy makers and education practitioners. In this sense, the Yuanmeng plans bore a resemblance to the large-scale illiteracy elimination education for workers and peasants in China in 1950s, which was 'endowed with a politico-symbolic and even spiritual significance' (Peterson 2001: 221). What is different between them, however, is that the emphasis on personal development was clearly perceived in the educational practices and discourses in the Yuanmeng plans. This had been supported by the then research findings of Zeng, Jia and He (2009). Their research suggests that nearly half of their interviewees (48.72 per cent) chose individual development as the major motive for training and continuing education (ibid). However, discourses of personal development appeared to have been overshadowed in the grand narratives of social and economic development.

What is noteworthy is that strong commercialism along with the practices of the socialist-planned economy was reflected in the discourse and implementation of the Yuanmeng plans. The Yuanmeng plans were planned and launched respectively by provincial government and municipal government. However, the implementation process, involving student recruitment and partnership institution selection, was commercialized involving different stakeholders. Discourses of socialism in education plans and guidelines were prominent. However, commercialism discourses were easily identified, for example 'well-known brand', 'intellectual property right' and 'fake brand' used in the Home of Migrants College's 'serious declaration' and official responses, as discussed earlier in this chapter. The incorporation of commercialism and socialism discourses constituted tensions in the practices of the Yuanmeng plans.

Some rules and practices led to the exclusion of certain migrant workers in need of continuing education and training such as Zhang Xiaohu and his teammates with lower literacy skills, as the Yuanmeng plans mainly offered academic degree courses. This can be related to an international trend that adult educational resources are often 'taken up by adults who have already benefited from formal schooling' (UNESCO 2015: 128). This means that some migrant workers would become more marginalized than those who engaged in educational opportunities such as the Yuanmeng plans. Bourdieu and Passeron claim that the educational system can be 'legitimating the reproduction of the social hierarchies by transmuting them into academic hierarchies' (1990: 152–3). In a similar vein, the Yuanmeng plans could be seen to increase the gap between migrant workers in terms of learning experiences, thus reshaping social norms and structures within migrant workers, and then normalizing the newly established social hierarchies.

4

Exploring the Teaching Force

When conducting participant observation with the Home of Migrants College, I first queried who was teaching, since there were a range of courses ranging from vocational training to degree courses, as introduced in Chapter 3. Likewise, I was interested in exploring how the Yuanda Yuanmeng Plan implemented its teaching as a provincial-scale campaign, which would need teachers in different subject areas.

In addition, I used to teach in China's universities but felt at a loss for how commercial educational institutions were being operated. Walking in the centre of Goods Town, Lychee City, I saw many stalls set up to recruit students for adult and online education, promising certificates to be conferred upon or boasting of wide social networks in running education. If I appeared to be curious, I would be stuck with persistent persuasion to join their programmes. Overdramatic descriptions of their teaching force were appealing to the audience.

There emerged a new term for trainers, 'training lecturers' (*peixun jiangshi* 培训讲师), in media. This teaching post did not exist in formal educational institutions, as the trainers were usually those who taught in commercial institutions. Some of them could be much more highly paid than the teachers in state-run schools and universities. Thus, their teaching contents and methods were vastly different from those in traditional teaching in that their eloquence and passion could ignite learners' enthusiasm.

This realization drove me to investigate how the teaching force was related to some other dimensions such as rules and events in the Yuanmeng plans. As mentioned in Chapter 2, Kabeer's Social Relations Framework (1994) places 'people' on a list of five dimensions: rules, resources, people, events and power. Accordingly, by what rules to select and manage teachers was analysed in line with the 'institutional patterns of inclusion, exclusion, placement and progress', as it incorporated implications concerning 'class, gender and other social patterns' (Kabeer 1994: 282). The concept of assemblage (Deleuze and Guattari 1987: 69) led me to analyse by what rules institutions and education workers were related to different institutions. The teaching forces as social actors were connected by discourses, power, resources and events on an assemblage; on this basis, some escaped from this assemblage and connected with a new assemblage.

Between 'our staff' and outside teachers

As mentioned above, the Home of Migrants College provided a variety of levels of courses, ranging from short-term vocational training and public lectures to long-term degree courses, whose degrees were awarded by supervising institutions outside Yuanda Province, as the Home of Migrants College had established partnerships with degree-awarding universities. Accordingly, the Home of Migrants College adopted comprehensive rules to select and place academic staff from both inside and outside the college to ensure its needs over a range of courses.

The exact number of universities recruiting students was slightly different from year to year. In the 2014 spring term, for instance, there were five partnership institutions from different provinces while there were four participating institutions in the 2013 spring term. The provided courses were of such different levels that the Home of Migrants College needed to guarantee its teaching staff would be qualified and responsible.

Teachers offering such courses as short-term vocational training and degree-awarding courses were mainly 'our own staff' in the words of Wang Shaogang, Vice President of this college. Those from outside the college mainly delivered public lectures to society and enterprises, although some of them taught short-term vocational training courses. However, as the academic education and degree courses were supervised by corresponding institutions outside Yuanda

Province, there were also online teachers, offering curriculum design, online teaching and supervision over the teaching process.

In explaining how 'our own staff' and the external teaching force were combined, Wang Shaogang introduced:

> We offer a diversity of short-term vocational training. We also give 400 lectures to the enterprises and factories annually. That means, every day we are giving more than a lecture somewhere in Haibin City, at enterprises or some other communities.... We contact the enterprises, or they contact us, for arranging lectures. The lecturers could be our own staff members or some well-known scholars. This maximizes the utilization of educational resources.
>
> (Interview notes with Wang Shaogang, 21 October 2012)

By 'maximizing the utilization of educational resources', as suggested by Wang Shaogang, the Home of Migrants College was able to include and exclude teaching staff according to its own criteria and needs, thus establishing a wide network of teaching resources. For instance, I encountered Li Ying in my fieldwork in the Home of Migrants College, who was teaching Property Management as a short-term vocational training course. Li Ying was holding a permanent teaching position in another college. He was also offering this course in other institutions in Haibin City. Having been working with the Home of Migrants College for a few years, as evidenced in college documents and brochures, Li Ying was included and progressed in this institution. Meanwhile, he formulated connections with different institutions and established different identities. The extensive teaching network enabled the Home of Migrants College to be socially influential. Thereby, this college was able to act as a platform where exchange of teaching force and knowledge was conducted.

The Home of Migrants College was constantly negotiating the relationship between 'our own staff' and external teaching staff in the implementation of its academic degree programmes. Teaching contents were prescribed by degree-awarding institutions. However, as assessment was conducted by the Home of Migrants College, but monitored by its supervising bodies, the local teaching force had enough power to administer the students' affairs of teaching and was authorized to conduct the whole teaching process.

The Home of Migrants College insisted on using its own instructors as its main teaching force in its degree courses. This was shown in my interview with Wang Shaogang, when I asked how they solved the issue of teaching force:

> All the teaching staff are from our own college. That is our condition for cooperating in the degree programmes. Otherwise, we would not collaborate with them. This ensures the sense of responsibility of the teaching staff. We believe education is to cultivate talents. Outsiders teaching temporarily cannot ensure the teaching quality as they cannot stay here always.
> (Interview notes with Wang Shaogang, 21 October 2012)

Wang Shaogang spoke very quickly so that he jumped from one thread of thought to another uninterrupted, although, occasionally, I stopped him for new questions. Wang's use of 'condition', 'collaborate', 'our' and 'outsiders' indicates that there had been a negotiation and power struggle between the Home of Migrants College and its partnership universities. The use of the local teaching force seemed to be the result of a compromise between the Home of Migrants College and its supervising universities, otherwise their students would receive only online instructions provided by degree-awarding universities. In this case, the value of the Home of Migrants College could not have been fully demonstrated. In this negotiation process, the supervising institutions acceded to the Home of Migrants College' education plans, as the Home of Migrants College provided resources of students and funding. They thus established stable partnerships.

By emphasizing the appointment of its own teachers in the degree courses for pedagogical practice as well as assessment, the Home of Migrants College asserted the value of its existence and highlighted its vital roles in the collaborative education projects. Meanwhile, its students received online teaching instructions from their respective degree-awarding universities and submitted online coursework. The Home of Migrants College taught its students and guided them until their graduation. They were, however, not labelled as the Home of Migrants College, but with the names of other institutions. Therefore, it seemed that they acted like processing plants: they made products, only to be labelled with the brands of other enterprises. Their students were satisfied with this arrangement. For instance, the students of the

Economic Management Class and the Machinery Engineering Class preferred to refer to themselves as the students from Beijing Skyline University, which would confer certificates on them.

The cooperation between the Home of Migrants College's own academics and those from its partnership universities shows that there existed a compromise between different educational institutions to survive in the education market. The Home of Migrants College was a lower rank educational institution; however, it was able to decide how the funding resources would be used. Thereby, it successfully included its own teaching force in the co-project force while excluded its supervising institutions from excessive interventions with its teaching. As a result, it restricted the external intervention with its teaching to some online pedagogical activities, which its students were supposed to attend. Education workers across different partnership institutions were able to be displaced and extended into different institutions. This contributed to their formulating assemblages with different actors and institutions. The Home of Migrants College won over some power from its supervising institutions, which, in turn, won economic and social benefits and resources, thus achieving power distribution and dynamic equilibrium.

Maintaining ideological consistency within teaching force

Different from the Haibin Yuanmeng Plan, the Yuanda Yuanmeng Plan assumed more complex configurations in its teaching force. As it was a provincial-level higher education programme for adult academic education, it was contracted by different educational institutions. Accordingly, its teaching force varied from city to city. I will focus on the teaching practice in Lychee City, as reflected in 'The Lychee City 2012 Working Proposal for Yuanda Yuanmeng Plan'. According to this plan, Lychee Waterfront University was designated as the only contractor of the Yuanda Yuanmeng education for Lychee City, as stated in Chapter 1.

As this programme was funded by a few departments of Yuanda Provincial Government and headed by Yuanda Communist Youth League, its teaching force was consolidated through promoting ideology and spiritual cultivation.

This is shown in the following specifications of this programme designed and practised in Lychee Waterfront University:

> Lychee Municipal Office of Yuanmeng Plan appoints a mentor for each class. This post, taken by an elite representative selected from all walks of social life, is intended to guide students to determine their ideals and beliefs, formulate correct attitudes towards life and sense of values, and encourage them to aspire higher. At the same time, Lychee Waterfront University appoints one mentor for each class, five tutors for academic learning and thirty learning assistants. The tutors for academic learning should be excellent teachers with strong sense of responsibility and good expertise. They are to help learners set up learning plans and cultivate good learning habits and scientific spirit. The learning assistants will be selected from distinguished undergraduates, postgraduates who are either in the middle of their courses or have graduated.... Besides, Lychee Municipal Communist League Committee appoints four to five assistants for the class mentor designated by Lychee Waterfront University. These assistants will be selected from the cadres of the Communist Youth League stationed in townships. They will help Lychee Municipal Office of the Yuanmeng Plan and class mentors with routine administration affairs, organize regular class activities, discover and cultivate model students, and guide them to become the backbones of the Party and Youth League.
>
> (Lychee Municipal Government 2012)

The above extract showed that human resources such as 'mentors' and 'tutors' ranging from municipal and township departments to university organizations were included to deepen the character cultivation of students by imparting the knowledge of the Communist Party and the Communist Youth League and consolidate the ideological leadership. As the major leader of this programme, the Communist Youth League raised funding and coordinated different social resources, and stressed the necessity of teaching relevant knowledge to the students.

Comparatively, the Home of Migrants College had in their courses' framework moral cultivation and character development, thought and politics, as required subjects in all state-run Chinese universities, as was mentioned in Chapter 3. Government administered departments, different from commercial and private institutions or enterprises, were in the framework of the System (*tizhi* 体制). Both being Yuanmeng plans sponsored by the government or by the System, emphasis on teaching mainstream socialist ideology appeared to be a natural result.

However, the dimension of thought and politics in the Yuanda Yuanmeng Plan in Lychee City was particularly stressed, as it advanced 'an elite representative' for each class and placed plenty of other human resources into this dimension of work. Lychee Waterfront University selected appropriate people from its own university human resources, including some full-time students. All involved planned to work together to enable the Yuanda Yuanmeng Plan students 'to become the backbones of the Party and Youth League'. Lychee City's prioritization of thought and politics in 2013 might be related to the fact that the Yuanda Yuanmeng Plan was a new and special task for them; meanwhile, the implementation of this plan was postponed until April 2013 while it should have been conducted in the latter half of 2012. Lychee Municipal Government, therefore, wanted to make this project a different one, and stressed even more the status of ideology and political training in its curriculum, thus allocating to this programme the teaching force selected from different institutions and enterprises.

The selection of teaching force to consolidate education on thought and politics in both the Yuanmeng plans resulted from the 'System'. In this System, government funding was secured yet more restrictions on 'who to teach what' were imposed. In the assemblage where education rules, education workers and resources were connected, emphasis on thought and politics was an important aspect of the projects. There appeared to exist a certain degree of ideological consolidation over the teaching force. Some people such as Zhao Daming, as will be mentioned below, who used to be in the System, chose to find 'a line of flight' (Deleuze and Guattari 1988: 9) and became freed from this field, and entered a commercial institution.

When 'working hard' as a doctrine did not work

In the Home of Migrants College, many teachers assumed more than one role and their working schedules were made in the way that there seemed to be no clear boundary between weekdays and weekends. Take for an example my gatekeeper, Xiao Zhiyuan. He was the director of the Department of Adult Education, in charge of the general administration affairs concerning part-time education while acting as the instructor of 'Rudiments of Management Science' in the 2013 Spring term. Even Wang Shaogang, Vice President of the Home of Migrants College, offered two subjects at the same time: Principles of Economics and Studies of Organizational Behaviour. All this work only referred to what they did over the weekends.

I was wondering how they distributed their time over the whole week. Later I realized that the major staff force was devoted to vocational education of full-time teenage students. This body of students was the focus of the Home of Migrants College. When needed for the weekend adult courses, some staff members would be assigned to support teaching and administration. Although only two days were arranged each week for adult education, this part of the work was extremely important in a sense. The registered part-time students outnumbered the full-time ones, and financially speaking, the education in this area brought more benefits to this college than the full-time education. This meant that the Home of Migrants College would mobilize all its staff for this cause in terms of student recruitment, teaching and coordination with external institutions and enterprises. Then it is no wonder many of the staff members shouldered multiple roles and their identities could be indefinite and fluid. The staff in the Department of Adult Education were especially busy that some of them continued working into the middle of July 2013 when most staff members in other departments had already begun their summer vacation.

It seemed that Wang Shaogang as well as the college authorities advocated that the staff should have sense of self-sacrifice for the collective benefit of the whole college, as shown in the following remark of Wang Shaogang when introducing staff composition:

'Our staff work intensively and carefully. We have strong sense of teamwork spirit'. I interrupted and asked: 'What if they have to work over the weekend? I mean they could sometimes work over the weekend. But what if they work habitually over the weekend? Will they complain?' Wang Shaogang replied: 'I often speak to my colleagues: "You would not lose much even if you work here, as you may waste a few hours at home doing nothing." Sometimes they can make extra cash for their work. However, it is nothing to be worthy of being mentioned. You see 50 yuan for one exam invigilation. That is nothing'.

(Interview notes with Wang Shaogang, 21 October 2012)

Wang Shaogang obviously made this point about their staff's general attitude towards work representing the college authorities. He used the word 'nothing' three times in this extract, which showed his confidence in his own judgement. He seemed to take it for granted that the staff should not complain even if they were asked to work over the weekend to take forward the college enterprise in the name of 'teamwork spirit'. It was from his own perspective, rather than from that of the staff member involved, that Wang Shaogang stated: 'you would not lose much, even if you work here, as you may waste a few hours at home doing nothing, as the relevant person could have thought about doing something more personal'.

I did not have any intention to gather complaints from the staff, as this might exert potential harm to their relationship. However, Zhao Daming's case served to prove something. I was not able to conduct a further interview about what Zhao Daming thought of the college administration. However, Zhao Daming's QQ online chat on 'training lecturers' appeared to show why he had decided to leave the Home of Migrants College:

Zhao Daming: Yesterday, I talked with a training lecturer, who makes as much as a few hundred thousand yuan a month. He put forward some profound ideas. Now I would like to share with you what I just learned from him.... A case study here. When someone says that you are stubborn, what would you think and do?

(QQ chat with Zhao Daming, 27 February 2014)

Before I analyse Zhao Daming's speech, I need to explain his changes in identity. As stated in Chapter 3, Zhao Daming used to be the mentor of the Class of Economic Management in the Home of Migrants College. But he had transferred to a new educational institution in Haibin when he made this remark above. I asked him where he was now, but he did not reply explicitly. I only knew he was working in a new training institution. I could not be sure if he was advertising for his new training programmes above, but there was a great degree of certainty that he was acting as a training lecturer or at least, he was planning to be one.

The shocking figure of 'a few hundred thousand yuan a month' was a farfetched figure for an ordinary education worker engaged in the formal educational system, such as the Home of Migrants College. But not every teacher could be a training lecturer, who seemed to be able to appeal to their audience in a commercial sense and teach them how to become a successful person in a competitive society, especially in terms of accumulating wealth, learning knowledge rapidly and acquiring expertise in a specific profession. This seemed to suggest that training lecturers were far away from the formal education system.

There seemed to exist a tension in working attitudes between the college authorities and the staff in the Home of Migrants College. To explain this tension, I will draw on Foucault's notion of power with two opposing tendencies. Foucault proposes two opposing tendencies of power: inertia and dynamism. The former refers to the normalizing and suppressing side of power while the latter refers to its liberating and productive side (Gordon 2020). The college authorities tended to take 'teamwork spirit' for granted, so everybody should be reconciled to it. They attempted to normalize their staff. However, some staff showed the dynamism of their own power. They were not involved in a face-to-face confrontation but utilized their capacity to enter a new area.

In discussing the workings of escape, Deleuze and Guattari put forward a nomadic principle of asignifying rupture: 'There is a rupture in the rhizome whenever segmentary lines explode into a line of flight' (1988: 9). This can be used to interpret how staff members such as Zhao Daming made a rupture from his original institution, took 'a line of flight' and transferred to a new place to be freed from being controlled. As discussed in Chapter 1, collectivism, hardworking and sacrifice were social ethos in Mao Zedong's times. However, such thoughts as sacrificing personal benefits for the general welfare of the working unit were not able to be fully accepted and were not taken as legitimate by all the individuals. This also indicated that changes in the subjectivities of the staff resulted from the combined factors and forces, notably institutional discourses and social actors, which will be further discussed in Chapter 7.

At this stage of China's social development with prevalent discourses of liberal marketing, when people had more mobility, such as Zhao Daming, they were dreaming of making big money and developing fully their personal career. Then it was not easy to make them work by simply advocating 'teamwork spirit'. They could manage to transgress the traditional boundary of the education system exerted by the state and switch to a new field. However, As Deleuze and Guattari warn: 'there is still a danger that you will reencounter organizations that restratify everything, formations that restore power to a signifier' (Deleuze and Guattari 1988: 9). The processes of flight 'are accompanied by a new form of priest and a new bureaucracy', thus being 'freed but still segmented, remaining negative and blocked' (ibid, 137). This suggests that there is no pathway for absolute flight from being controlled – the flight from one institution is always leading to another one involving hierarchical power. With this idea explaining the dialectical relationship between flight and control, I have understood that Zhao Daming, though freed from an institution, were then controlled by a new commercial organization featured with social and economic hierarchies. He had to work harder to promote his new educational products to aspire for a higher material and social status.

Connections, assemblages and flight

This chapter investigated the teaching force for the Yuanmeng plans. It explored how far the teaching force was socially constituted, included, excluded, placed and advanced. My analysis shows that the teaching force in the Home of Migrants College assumed a complex configuration. The major feature was close interconnection with external society while dispelled excessive intervention from other partnership institutions. This helped maintain the independence of its own staff and ensured its value and vigour, thus gaining a sense of identity and material benefits.

While both the Yuanmeng plans were highly aligned in thought and politics with the Communist Party of China by offering relevant subjects, the practice in Lychee Waterfront University placed extra emphasis on the Party and Youth League knowledge by appointing human resources in this project. Likewise, the attitudes of the leadership and its staff in the Home of Migrants College towards the discourse of collective 'teamwork spirit' pointed to the fact that the young generation of the staff would not be bound by this thought. To realize their own ideals and aspiration, they chose to take a different path, assisted with external social resources. This way, they stayed away from the traditional boundary of the 'System'.

The study of the teaching force in the Yuanmeng plans has shown that adult education projects involved various human resources. Authorities attempted to align them to dominating social and educational ideology such as collective welfare and selfless devotion. However, ordinary teaching staff began to change their mindset with the influence of liberal marketing and commercialism. Thereby, a dynamic relation between educational and governmental authorities and the teaching force seemed to have been shaped.

5

Exploring Pedagogical Practice

I started teaching English to degree courses in the Home of Migrants College in March 2013, as mentioned earlier. Xiao Zhiyuan, my gatekeeper, asked me to study the handbook for staff for the general requirements and the guidance for students and staff.

As stated in Chapter 1, to guarantee my teaching, the key administrators in charge of the Haibin Yuanmeng Plan organized a meeting with me. Those present were Xiao Zhiyuan, my gatekeeper, Chen Yi, director of the general affairs of adult education in the Home of Migrants College, Zhou Li, coordinator of online and distant learning, and Zhao Daming, mentor of the Economic Management Class. Every one of them intently imparted to me the major points. They stressed the importance of interactive teaching, assessment methods and strict attendance registration.

The meeting was informative but fragmented for me. From time to time, there appeared to be disagreements between them, as there were some new rules made, with which not everybody was familiar. Soon afterwards, I received a written notice from Chen Yi on 'Supplementary rules for teaching administration of the Yuanmeng Plan academic degree courses'. This notice, in comparison with the teaching handbook from Xiao Zhiyuan, was more practically orientated. These rules mapped out the teaching process: students' assignments, drafting mock test papers by students, attendance registration, methods of assessment, teaching methods and teaching assessment. These 'supplementary' rules lent support to understanding the key points in the education administration, teaching and assessment. 'Supplementary' itself indicated that rules were added based on the formal Yuanmeng handbook. As will be played out, the teaching documents and the pedagogical practices constituted significant tensions and contradictions between policy and its implementation.

The rest of this chapter explores how the teaching and administration of courses were conducted in the Haibin Yuanmeng Plan. In addition, the findings from the Yuanda Yuanmeng Plan are used to make a comparative analysis. I will start with the concept of 'hidden curriculum' as a lens to explore the tension between the 'didactic curriculum' as 'an explicit, conscious, formally planned course' and 'an unwritten curriculum', which is hidden curriculum, 'described by informality and lack of conscious planning' (Kentli 2009). I wish to examine the tensions embedded between these education plans and their actual practice. I will focus on 'an evaluation of the environment and the unexpected, unintentional interactions between teachers and students' (ibid). On this basis, I will use the Deleuzian concept of assemblage as a lens and analyse how these interactions as events were connected with other heterogeneous factors, such as institutional rules and resources, and what results these connections produced.

Between actual and virtual spaces

As stated earlier in this book, online educational activities were an indispensable part of the Yuanmeng plans. In some institutions, all the teaching procedures were conducted online. While digital technologies were de-institutionalizing the traditional teaching, institutions such as the Home of Migrants College seemed to suggest that face-to-face learning was more 'real' and more effective.

Some of the institutions in the Yuanda Yuanmeng Plans espoused pure distance learning, as supported by Chuan Aixiang's case. As mentioned in Chapter 3, Chuan Aixiang was a distance-learning student funded by the Yuanda Yuanmeng Plan. Registered with Hubei Innovative University in Wuhan City, Hubei Province, he had all his learning conducted online except formal examinations when invigilation from relevant administrations was given on the site of an agency in Haibin City. He told me a story via a QQ interview about his online viva for his graduation:

Me: How did you do your viva?
Chuan Aixiang: Through internet interview.

Me: It seems that everything is being internetized now.

Chuan Aixiang: Yes, our education programme is also high-tech supported. We used web viva on the platform of the internet. I was lucky as I almost failed to be allowed to participate in this viva. I missed the deadline for getting registered for this year and had to wait for next year. But I adopted 'viva of violence'.

Me: What do you mean?

Chuan Aixiang: I was present at the viva meeting where judges and students were interviewing. At the end of the session, the judges asked if there were any questions. I used the opportunity to report my problem and entreated them to give me a chance. So, I got it. That was just incredible. I passed the viva and is going to receive my bachelor's degree soon.

(Online interview with Chuan Aixiang, 16 June 2013)

The use of the internet had become an indispensable means in the Yuanda Yuanmeng Plan. It was not only a channel through which teaching was conducted, but also a platform where interactions involving students, instructors and administrators conducted their administrative activities. So Chuan Aixiang was resourceful enough to reverse the situation in which he would have to postpone his graduation time.

However, educational agencies and institutions mainly engaged in online education usually included some amount of face-to-face teaching. This helped establish a social and educational network, which acted as a platform integrating virtual with actual spaces. Interviewing an administrator of Lychee Seabreeze Academy under the Yuanda Yuanmeng Plan, as stated in Chapter 1, I noticed that this teaching site provided only a very limited number of subjects on the education of thought and politics while all the other specialty subjects were conducted online. However, as mentioned in Chapter 1, in April 2013, Lychee Municipal Government designated Lychee Waterfront University as its only contractor in Lychee City for the Yuanda Yuanmeng Plan, which offered face-to-face teaching for this programme.

In the case of the Home of Migrants College, although it insisted on providing face-to-face teaching to its students, it left online teaching to its partnership institutions such as Beijing Skyline University. This rendered its students more learning opportunities. However, online practice had become an indispensable channel for information sharing, reflected not only in its teaching but also in its administration process. I will describe some events of my first teaching in this college to illustrate the tension between online and face-to-face teaching:

> The first two sessions were given to the Class of Economic Management. Zhou Li, in charge of the general affairs of distance learning, introduced me warmly to the students and said they should treasure this chance to learn from me. There are over 140 students in this class, scattered over four teaching sites. Through a screen, I saw students on the other three sites, which were in large scale enterprises. As quite a percentage of the students in this class were from these enterprises, they cooperated with the Home of Migrants College in establishing teaching sites for the convenience of the students. There were around 80 students on the major site, where I was lecturing, while students on the other three sites attended the sessions through telecommunication. I felt rather nervous at the beginning, for I did feel a loss at how to interact with the other three sites. I became completely confused when calling the roll, as it was time consuming for 140 students over four sites.
>
> (Fieldwork notes, 03 March 2013)

While the Home of Migrants College stressed the importance of face-to-face education practice for the online teaching programmes supervised by its partnership institutions, it turned to telecommunication technology for its pedagogical practice. The teaching of English to the Economic Management Class on its campus was transmitted to another three teaching sites in the same city. Thus, there appeared an integration of distance and face-to-face education, or blended learning, as a dominating practice in the degree programmes in this college.

That afternoon on the same day, I delivered a few sessions to the Class of Machinery Manufacturing. Then I came to understand further the complicated relationship between the Home of Migrants College and its supervising institutions. Ninety per cent of the students in this class were male.

> They were very talkative, unlike those in the morning who were just listening. In the break of the afternoon sessions, Huang Yan, class mentor, came in and called up a class meeting. She told me that they would like to have a class meeting during the break. Huang Yan introduced to her students the platform which was the only official website for students to log in for distance learning. 'It is a supermarket like Tesco. Many businesses there.

The centre of our college is just one of their clients. We are controlled by them or working together with them'.

(Fieldwork notes, 03 March 2013)

Huang Yan's vivid explanation to her students employing words such as 'Tesco' and 'client' exposes a commercial attribute in its education programme, which involved several stakeholders, co-linked by virtual and actual spaces to make profits.

All the events and scenarios, pasted together, present a picture where there were interwoven and interconnected virtual spaces and actual spaces through both traditional and digital technologies. However, what I knew about the students was still fragmented, as the class on the first day was most of the time quiet, monotonous and eventless. By the end of the day, Wen Xiangyang, a student from the Machinery Engineering Class, as mentioned in Chapter 2, who seemed to be concerned about my mission as a researcher, told me to join their online chatroom: 'You will know everything about us from there, if you want to study us'. (Fieldwork notes, 03 March 2013)

Surprisingly, after the first day of sessions, in the class virtual chatrooms, in which students and relevant staff members joined, chatroom members were engaged in heated discussions. Some even used English especially for the first few days after this semester started, practising English while sharing information. This was most likely inspired by their first day English sessions and by me being present. Some students did not like it, saying that they should use Chinese as most were not good at English.

It seemed that, therefore, internet resources played multiple roles. They provided an important platform, where pedagogical practices were implemented, and acted as a social network, where students shared information and consolidated friendship that had started in the daytime. In addition, they acted as an important channel through which to receive notices of the Haibin Yuanmeng Plan from the education administrations and instructors.

Digital technologies brought great benefits and conveniences to students and educators in the education practice of both the Yuanmeng plans. Consequently, online education became a dominant form in these programmes. However, there existed a resistance against this trend, as shown in the case of the Home of Migrants College. As stated in Chapter 4, this College stressed utilizing its own teaching force in its degree programmes, which were monitored by its supervising partnership institutions. Likewise, to assert its relative autonomy, the Home of Migrants College was adamant that it would conduct face-to-face pedagogical practice among its students. Paradoxically, it applied online teaching to other sites, whereby it was able to employ fully the resources of its teaching and facilities to more students, thus making connections with other institutions.

The Home of Migrants College was thereby engaged in both face-to-face and distance teaching. This embodied a Deleuzian ontological world, as defined by DeLanda, 'a world of actual individual entities (nested within one another at different spatio-temporal scales), produced by intensive individuation processes, themselves governed by virtual multiplicities' (2004: 64). This was a world, which was populated a heterogeneity of factors: institutional rules on teaching formats and teaching events, social actors such as students and teachers, and tangible and intangible educational resources. From the interactions of these factors, power negotiations were progressing. The Home of Migrants College adopted a flexible means by which to negotiate its identity and maintain its prosperity on the competitive education market, thus displaying the value of its existence as an educational institution. This will be further illustrated in the following section on how attendance registration was conducted and why I was nervous when calling the roll.

When strict attendance registration was not always observed

As mentioned earlier in this chapter, a requirement for strict attendance registration and roll call was stipulated in the Home of Migrants College as a compulsory procedure of teaching administration. From time to time, I observed there were sheets of name list circulating in classrooms for signing; otherwise, there would be a roll call instead. As it was such a routine scenario, I will analyse how attendance registration was prescribed in the curriculum plan and how it was implemented.

> Attendance registration was prescribed in 'Yuanmeng Plan academic education manual': Instructors should be responsible for students' attendance registration and require students to sign on registration sheets. Student

cannot sign for others or put in late entry… As for the students on distance learning, instructors need to call the roll at irregular intervals and ensure attendance registration.

(the Yuanmeng Plan Academic Education Manual 2012)

On this basis, 'Supplementary rules for teaching administration of the Yuanmeng Plan academic degree courses' (Haibin Yuanmeng Plan documents 2013), as mentioned earlier in this chapter, put forward a concrete rule: 'The attendance rate will be taken as a part accounting for 30% of the total mark'. This measure directly linked students' attendance rates with their final scoring.

Students' attendance registration was directly related to the strict administration for adult education in the Home of Migrants College. This can be clearly seen from Vice President, Wang Shaogang's article, published on their official website, and it shows why this college placed strict rules on students' administration:

> It is an effective measure to implement strict teaching administration and stress exam disciplines. This will pass on a clear signal to those poor-quality applicants…. The Yuanmeng Plan, unlike some other educational institutions, is strict with teaching administration. Its essence is to take responsibility for students and Trade Union. From the very day when the students get admitted, normative education and disciplines are exerted so that the students will have their behaviour normalized to attain the goal of Trade Union: developing migrant workers into 'new workers and new citizens of Haibin City' and helping the hard-working people realize their Chinese Dreams.
>
> (Wang Shaogang's speech 2012)

Wang Shaogang linked the strict rules and strict administration for the Haibin Yuanmeng Plan with the goal set by the Haibin Trade Union, the sponsor of this programme. He particularly pointed out 'some other educational institutions' as a contrast to the Home of Migrants College. This alluded to other rapidly developing adult education programmes and institutions in Yuanda Province. To say no to the 'poor quality applicants' for the Haibin Yuanmeng Plan, Wang used a line of discourse: 'strict', 'discipline', 'responsibility', 'normative' and 'develop' to achieve the goals represented by a line of discourse such as 'the Chinese Dream', 'new workers' and 'new citizens'. This reflected his strict guidelines in running the Haibin Yuanmeng Plan by evoking students' sense of aspiration and integrating patriotism with personal goals. It followed that rigid attendance registration was introduced as a most effective means by which to monitor teaching and students' affairs.

The idea of being strict with students' administration was deeply rooted in the staff's mind. In the group meeting with the key figures in the Home of Migrants College, as mentioned above, the importance of observing rigidly attendance registration and roll call was reiterated, as Chen Yi, in charge of general affairs in adult education in the Home of Migrants College, warned me: 'It would be least desirable if one teacher is strict with attendance registration while another one is not, if they teach the same class'.

However, while addressing attendance registration on my first teaching day, I encountered embarrassing moments:

> At the end of the two sessions to the Class of Economic Management, when I was ready to call the roll, I found that things were not that easy. There were over 140 students over four sites. The students in the major teaching site signed their names, as a rule. But as for the other three teaching sites, I would need to call the roll one by one. The names on the sheet did not show which site the students were on. I asked Zhao Daming, class mentor, who had already come in, to help me. He said: 'Just do it. That is all right. Try more. You will do it next time as well'. I felt a bit awkward when hearing that. To call the roll was truly time consuming, but I had to. However, the students having done their roll call started to stand up and move about while some others were waiting to be called.
>
> (Fieldwork notes, 03 March 2013)

I came to learn how to call the roll, and when: never do this at the end of my sessions but do it at the beginning or in the middle of them. Otherwise, there would be a rush to do it. As I gained more experiences in this college as a teacher, something unexpected gradually grabbed my attention when I was conducting attendance registration. When I shouted the names of some students, I was told that they would not have to come. As they were self-funded students rather than sponsored by the Haibin Yuanmeng Plan, they could be absent and teach themselves on condition that they signed an agreement with the college, promising they would conduct learning online but take the same tests as other students. But in case one did not sign the agreement, they had to ensure regular attendance. This was clarified by my online interview with the class representative, Zhao Rong, as shown below:

> Zhao Rong: Some students have signed an agreement with the college saying they would teach themselves rather than attend classes. They are self-funded students, so they are allowed to be absent from class.
> Me: Then many students could choose to teach themselves via online teaching rather than attend weekend classes. This means they would be out of the control of college disciplines.
> Zhao Rong: Yes, as some students were not happy with the decision that class attendance be required.... It would be hard to comment on this. We have different purposes here. Some people do want to learn something while some others simply want a certificate. So, there are no strict requirements for self-funded students, but the Yuanmeng funded students are required to register their attendances and accumulate phased assessment over the whole study period.
>
> (Online interview with Zhao Rong, 05 May 2013)

The realization that there existed different rules for students' attendance was further deepened when I attempted to confirm it with Chen Yi, in charge of the general affairs of adult education in the Home of Migrants College. As I was attending to strict attendance registration, I asked her if she should pass on to me the information of those who were allowed to be absent from class. Chen Yi did not appear to be interested in my request, saying that it would be all right if I did not have this name list and I just did my work well. This meant that I should be very careful with the attendance registration, as it would be a failure of duty if someone absent was documented as present or vice versa. This involved a lot of work and energy, especially in the case of the Class of Economic Management with over 140 students.

As stated above, 'some students were not happy' with the class attendance. They took alternative paths to deal with this rule. More than once, quite a few students on the major teaching site had left earlier than scheduled, as the roll call had been completed. The other teaching sites were even harder to control. Although required to face the web camera all throughout the sessions, they were not easy to monitor. Sometimes, I would call the roll more than once to ensure their presence, as I found quite a percentage of the students were absent. Absenteeism became a serious problem, which proved why the

Home of Migrants College emphasized the importance of strict college rules and attendance registration. This phenomenon will be picked up again later in Chapter 6 on extracurricular activities.

Therefore, the Home of Migrants College employed rigid attendance registration as the most immediate way to exert discipline over its students. This could be an effective measure for teaching and learning administration in the age of overwhelming online education. As mentioned earlier in this chapter, Kentli (2009) explains 'hegemony' and 'resistances' as two conflicting tendencies in implementing curriculum. This could be linked with the relationship between the college administration and its students in the curriculum practice with the Home of Migrants College. It was inconsistent that the Haibin Yuanmeng Plan-funded students would have to attend but self-funded ones would not. The key to this compromise rested with the difference whether funding supply was given or not. If a recipient accepted the funding, they would need to attend their teaching sessions. Otherwise, they would be allowed to be absent. The Home of Migrants College was dominated by high-profile discourses: 'new workers', 'new citizens' and 'the Chinese Dream', as stated in Wang Shaogang's article. These discourses were used to inspire migrant students to be committed to their learning and observe college rules; meanwhile, funding as a way of material resource was also adopted to bind them. However, the Home of Migrants College had reconciled to resistant actions from self-funded students, thus giving them alternatives to attending face-to-face sessions.

'Let's have some interaction'

In the Home of Migrants College, students' participation was stressed as a part of pedagogical process. Various measures were taken to put this idea to practise. This was reflected in such aspects as education policies, teaching process and teaching strategies. As mentioned above, in 'Supplementary rules for teaching administration of the Yuanmeng Plan academic degree courses', several measures were blueprinted to encourage students' involvement in teaching and learning. The most direct one was the use of 'teaching method of exploration and increase interactions between students and teachers. Teachers are encouraged to go down to the sub-branch teaching sites to provide guidance for students' queries'. Both the teachers and the learners appeared to have been entrenched in such ideas as interactions between students and teachers.

The impact of interactive teaching was reflected in the inconsistency between the curriculum design and its actual practice in the Home of Migrants College, or in the tensions and contradictions between 'the didactic curriculum' and 'an unwritten curriculum' (Kentli 2009). More than once, I noted that teachers mentioned 'interaction' about their pedagogical practice. The following episodes concerned three teachers: Li Ying, Liang Meijing and Wang Shaogang from different subjects.

Li Ying, as stated in Chapter 4, had been teaching the subject of property management in the Home of Migrants College. This course was allocated over ten days across a period of two months. Those who passed qualifying tests would be issued certificates for conservators of property management. I had observed Li Ying's class for three whole days, which lasted from 9:30 am until 5 pm on Sundays. On the first day, he did not expect me to remain in his classroom after lunch break, as I noticed his surprised look when our eyes met. He explained by the end of my first observation: 'You see the course material is very professional and can be boring. So, I tried to remember the name of each student and encouraged them to be engaged in class discussion, thus strengthening class interaction' (Interview notes with Li Ying, 25 November 2012).

Li Ying seemed to know almost everyone and called out their names. For instance, Liang Dazhi, an aspiring student in this class and an employee with a property management company, always sat in the first row, responding and questioning. Sometimes, Li Ying played a harmless joke on him, as Liang Dazhi was an agreeable man and never got offended. Li Ying's emphasis on 'class interaction' indicated that, as a researcher, I should be most concerned about his teaching method, and that, as a teacher, he had attempted to be interactive.

Likewise, Liang Meijing showed her anxiety with the idea of 'interaction'. Liang Meijing, around thirty years old, was a teacher of English for a class majoring in electronic engineering supervised by Tianjing Haihe University in

Tianjin City. I observed twice Liang Meijing's English teaching. The following was focused on the second observation:

> It was 1 pm. After the whole morning sessions, students looked tired. I perceived that she was balancing the relationship between teaching, students' levels in English, and the management from the supervisory university and the education authorities.... The whole class was examination centred. Most of the time, she explained practices in the form of multiple choices, and announced answers like 'A, boy, C and dog'. I soon realized that 'boy' stands for 'B' and 'dog' for 'D'. The students and the teacher seemed to have reached mutual understanding and much cooperation in practice and analysis. There were about 75 students present. English was to be tested as a condition for their graduation. The students and the teacher negotiated over teaching material and exam content, as they would have an exam of English administered by Tianjin Haihe University, their supervisory institution in Tianjin City. Liang Meijing seemed to be confident about what to be tested, as she ensured her students that most of them would get marks over 75 if they worked hard enough so that they could have the chance to sit English degree exam given by the provincial level authority.
>
> (Fieldwork notes, 16 December 2012)

Liang Meijing's class was exam orientated and text focused. English would be tested if one wanted to apply for a bachelor's degree, but the qualifying test would be given by a provincial level test committee. So the teaching of English was targeted at two goals. The first goal was a primary one, for graduation, and the second one, which was harder, was only for those intending to apply for a bachelor's degree. The teaching contents in this class were more controlled by test practice and analysis. One of Liang Meijing's catchphrases was 'Do you understand what I mean?' This seemed to convey her sense of inward uncertainty about her teaching efficiency. Also, she said a couple of times, 'Everybody is like this. We cannot achieve anything if we are not forced to work hard'. By this, Liang Meijing encouraged her students to work hard under pressure.

Interestingly, Liang Meijing could be the age of her students or even younger than many of them, she showed her loving care to them as if they were much younger pupils. She warned: 'No cheating in exams. You will be failed automatically'. Thus, Liang Meijing lectured throughout while her students listened and took notes, as her teaching contents were on test papers for graduation. She explained to me by the end of the class which lasted until 6:00 pm:

> 'Today, I was teaching them test contents and testing methods, so maybe not much for you to see'. I said: 'You did very well. But I am not here to make judgment about your teaching effectiveness. I am just interested in students' situations, education and life. Hope you did not mind my presence'. 'You are an experienced teacher. I should learn from you'. 'Oh, no. you did do very well. OK, let's learn from each other'. We both laughed to stop this mutual flattering.
>
> (Fieldwork notes, 16 December 2012)

Liang Meijing attempted to clarify why her teaching was not 'interactive'. She seemed to feel guilty as I had not observed 'interactive' activities.

The third scenario is from Wang Shaogang, Vice President of the Home of Migrants College. The afternoon sessions began at 1 pm o'clock, and I arrived there a bit earlier. I was surprised that Wang Shaogang could give such inspiring and attractive lectures on this subject as I know he majored in mechanics or a relevant area. Today's topic was on 'encouragement and masses'. He encouraged his students to reflect by raising a question: 'Can money solve every problem?' The students responded, 'No'. Wang Shaogang said, 'But nobody would be happy if they are owed a cent'. Wang Shaogang started his lecture with a thought-provoking question to grab his students' attention. It was hard to sustain students' attention throughout his long lecture, as shown below:

> The classroom was filled with his voice. He then discussed various theories of management, and very often he connected his theories with the cases around manufacturing in Haibin City. Wang Shaogang then continued to introduce other schools of management theories. It was stuffy and hot in the classroom. Some students were dozing off. This could be understood as they had been here from 9:30 am. Some had to leave home as early as 6:00 am in order not to be late. Wang Shaogang then walked down from the platform and said: 'Let's have some interaction'. He walked up to a male student and asked: 'Can you please say something about Maslow's theory on demand?' The student answered embarrassedly: 'Sorry. I don't know'. 'Then go back to read for it and learn something'.
>
> (Fieldwork notes, 09 December 2012)

Wang was concerned to engage his students in interaction. He started his lecture with a question, prompting reflection and interaction from his students. In the middle of his lecture, he went down from the platform to interact with his students. 'Let's have some interaction' was very revealing as it seemed to let it be known to everyone present, including outsiders such as me as an observer that interactive and explorative methods were employed in their pedagogical practice. However, 'go back to read for it and learn something' was more of a warning and penalization for the ignorant student who had already felt 'sorry' but not an invitation for interaction, as he immediately resumed his lecture.

The above described how the discourse around 'interactive' teaching held sway over the teachers in the Home of Migrants College. To develop the idea of interactive method in my own pedagogical practice, on my first day of teaching with the Class of Economic Management, I asked students to introduce themselves, as a way of 'interaction'. They seemed to be expecting the traditional university life, consisting of classmates, fun, activities, books and discussion rather than boring videos and static signs typical of distance education, as described below:

> In the stage of students' self-introduction, the students recommended one young man, named Zheng Zhiyong, to represent the whole class and said something. He started in English, 'How do you do?' Some people laughed. Zheng Zhiyong turned to Chinese immediately, 'Maybe I am not a good image for Wall Street'. Some laughed understandingly, but I was puzzled and asked: 'What is Wall Street?' Zheng Zhiyong continued: 'It is an institution for training English in Haibin City. I am not doing ad for them, by the way'. One asked: 'How much is the tuition fee?' 'Twenty thousand yuan'. (two thousand pounds or so) 'You are rich', exclaimed someone jokingly.
>
> (Fieldwork notes, 03 March 2013)

Zheng Zhiyong, as he himself admitted, was not a good image for 'Wall Street', as the only English expression 'How do you do', which he used as a symbolical act for the English class, was out of date. While I did not have sufficient knowledge of 'Wall Street' as an English training institution, Zheng Zhiyong's classmates obviously knew about it, as they were quickly responsive to his speech. I would understand Zheng Zhiyong's remark was not purposefully put, but to fill up the gap that he was asked to 'say something' as a class representative. However, in his subtext, English could be important for their career, and 'Wall Street' English could be more helpful than what we were doing here. This made me guilty as their teacher of English, as the commercially run courses were more influential on these students. Zheng Zhiyong was an adventurous and ambitious young man, who would establish an electronic company in early 2015, as he announced this news in the virtual chatroom and invited his classmates of the Yuanmeng Plan to an opening ceremony.

As the class mentioned 'Wall Street', we then discussed the methods that many commercial training schools were employing: 'Meili, in her thirties, answered immediately, "passionate and interactive". I was surprised she should be so familiar with the saying and discourses in this sort of institutions, as indeed this was a catchphrase I had heard of' (Fieldwork notes, 03 March 2013).

As stated at the beginning of Chapter 4, 'training lecturers' were appealing to learners on the courses provided by commercially run institutions. So Meili and Zheng Zhiyong provided examples to the influence of such institutions on students and public, whose emblem was 'passionate' and 'interactive'. Their responses also indicated that what we were doing was not interactive. If so, I did not fulfil the 'supplementary rules' on interactive teaching as prescribed by the Home of Migrants College. Passionate or interactive, for the Home of Migrants College, implied 'updated and advanced'. If there was no passion or interaction involved in teaching, then it was an inappropriate teaching and learning experience.

Clearly, the Home of Migrants College stressed the importance of pedagogy, as shown in its documents and classroom activities. This finding could be linked with Kelly's (2009: 13) observation in the research contextualized in the UK education: 'The focus of evaluation has moved from a concern with the value of what is being offered to a concentration on the effectiveness of its "delivery"'. In the Home of Migrants College, interactive teaching was promoted by teaching principles and prompted by nominating students to answer questions. However, what was prescribed seemed to be discrepant from its practice, which largely remained teacher-centred, disengaging the students from interactions. Thereby, there emerged a contradiction between the obsession with the concept of interactive pedagogical practice and the actual employment of the teacher-centred approach.

Tensions between written curriculum and unwritten curriculum

This chapter explored the curriculum practice of migrant workers' education in the Haibin Yuanmeng Plan. It focused on the tension between written and formal curriculum and unwritten and hidden curriculum to examine what was promoted and what was implemented.

First, emphasis on strict attendance registration, even at the 'sacrifice' of teaching time, showed that the educational institution intended to administer students rigidly. However, the inconsistency in treating students with different funding sources reflected the effect of commercialization. The college was reconciled with the self-funded students and exempted them from face-to-face sessions. However, the Yuanmeng-funded students needed to ensure their presence in class and their general performance like attendance rates and assignments would be documented as part of their final score. This meant that one would have to observe the college's rules on attendance when accepting the government's funding. While discourses such as 'the Chinese Dream', 'new citizens' and 'new workers' were used to inspire students, the self-funded ones were relieved of the rules on class attendance. This result shows that the college was bent to the influence of commercialization. Consequently, some students took 'a line of flight' (Deleuze and Guattari 1988: 9) through commercialization from the disciplines of the college and entered a new assemblage. The Haibin Yuanmeng Plan for 2020 has retained the discourses around the Chinese Dream, new citizens and new workers, as will be picked up in Chapter 9. On a national level, the tension between the discourses around socialist ideology and the practices related to commercialization seems to be noticeable. Against this background of increasingly commercialized society, Xi Jinping (2020), the president of China, calls on the education of patriotism, socialism and collectivism to consolidate national cohesion in ideology and social practice, as stated in Chapter 1.

In addition, the Home of Migrants College stressed the use of interaction in teaching, as prioritized in their written curriculum. However, its practice largely remained teacher dominated. This was shown in the contradictions between its strict disciplines and actual classroom practice. The teaching involving interactions between teachers and students appeared to be symbolically implemented. Interestingly, the insistence on interactive teaching, as shown with the teachers and their official documents, was clear. Meanwhile, some students such as Zheng Zhiyong and Meili expected learning activities where passion could be fully displayed. This dilemma could be related to the educational trend since the start of the twenty-first century, as EFA Global Monitoring Report (UNESCO 2015) observed: 'The past decade has seen a move away from teacher-dominated instructional practices to learner-centred pedagogy. But implementation can be difficult. Challenges include a lack of supportive environments, teacher training and preparation, textbooks and teaching materials, and too-large class sizes' (42). The pedagogical practice described in this report had emerged in the Home of Migrants College: an increasing tendency towards student-centred teaching from teacher-centred teaching, which, however, was hindered by various factors, notably the large-sized class in my study. Although discourses, such as official documents and ideas of students and teachers, were focused on interaction and passion, what happened in the pedagogical practice was more orientated by a traditional textbook-focused and exam-orientated approach. Thereby, traditional pedagogical practice espousing conformity and collectivism existed side by side with new pedagogical practice advocating individualism and interaction.

Thirdly, the Home of Migrants College insisted on face-to-face education to show their value and power. Without active engagement in the process of teaching, which could have been fulfilled online by other institutions, they were afraid that they could not have demonstrated their existence. Thereby, the Home of Migrants College was faced with the dilemma of competing with digital technologies while making use of them. The outbreak of the Covid-19 impacted social and economic development on a global scale. I was, thus, pushed to rethink the controversy over digital technologies, as shown with the Home of Migrants College.

While I was writing this book, the pandemic started to spread worldwide. This severely disturbed the learning and the teaching of all levels ranging from primary school to higher education. This event enormously augmented people's reliance on the internet, which played a vital role in connecting people, resources, events and other heterogenous factors. This unprecedentedly foregrounded the importance of digital technologies for online education. The advantage of online education could thus be fully demonstrated when faced with the Covid-19 pandemic, as it enabled 'educators and students to continue teaching and learning from any location without interruption' and ensured sustained profit to educational institutions (Vlachopoulos 2020: 17).

However, challenges for online education existed in social, economic and technological aspects, for example untested or inconsistently applied new measures (Vlachopoulos 2020), inadequate monitoring, assessment and evaluation mechanisms (Adedoyin and Soykan 2020; Vlachopoulos 2020), unreliable and unequal access to online technology and resources, and incompatibility with some disciplines (Adedoyin and Soykan 2020). The challenges made me reflect, as online learning had become the only option and would remain so for an uncertain period, how educational stakeholders should be adjusted to changing circumstances and make online learning and teaching effective, validated and accredited.

In the middle of the pandemic, I was employed to teach an academic subject to students with a UK university, all learning, teaching, assessment and accreditation conducted online. I realized that, different though this teaching experience was from my previous ones, educational activities, at least for social sciences in higher education, were able to continue. Though face-to-face contact in the teaching process had been reduced, we remained on an assemblage populated by social actors, teaching resources, events, rules, power and affect. We experienced feelings such as excitement, anxiety, happiness and regrets. We were still located in a Deleuzian 'interworld' (Bogue 1989: 54), where actual spaces and virtual spaces were interpenetrating and interconnecting.

This pedagogy featured with overwhelming online events foregrounded the indispensable role of digital technologies, which have enabled many more learners to access teaching recourses than traditional educational institutions. Thus, as Wang and Chen (2021) argue that, in their study of migrant workers' education in China, that traditional classroom-based learning pedagogy be changed and multiple modes of learning be adopted by means of digital technologies. This understanding could be linked with the recommendation by UNESCO (2020: 8) on the future of education and lifelong learning: digital technology should be placed 'at the service of lifelong learning for all' and 'Towards 2050 – digital learning technology for the common and the public good' should be launched. In addition, the trend of dominating online learning points to the necessity of adopting multiple modes of learning with rapidly transformed educational institutions. This idea will be further analysed in Chapter 8 regarding the relationships between formal, informal and nonformal learning.

In conclusion, the Home of Migrants College endeavoured to bring in new pedagogical ideas and practices; however, traditional values and practices were still impacting the new practices. Consequently, tensions and contradictions of events and discourses emerged between traditional face-to-face teaching and online teaching, between traditional socialist ideology and modern commercialism, and between interactive teaching and traditional text-focused teaching. These tensions and contradictions will be further analysed in the subsequent chapters on how students' extracurricular activities and assessment of students were conducted.

6

Exploring Outward Development

In the Home of Migrants College, collective extracurricular activities were advocated. 'Outward development' (*tuozhan xunlian* 拓展训练) was one of them. The following is an excerpt from a report on an outward development implemented in this college:

> Through this outward development, three aims have been realised. Firstly, this training programme helped all the 73 students in the Yuanmeng Plan understand themselves, stimulate personal potential, objectively orientate themselves, promote their confidence and confront the challenges of work and life. Secondly, through communications between different levels of awarding institutions and classes, the students have learned to improve interrelationships, care for, encourage and trust in their peers, and to cooperate with others harmoniously. Thirdly, the training system of the Yuanmeng Plan has been further improved. Based on the specialty teaching and studying, the outward development integrating different classes helped cultivate the students' personal comprehensive competencies, broaden their communicative channels, and promote their ability to discover, understand and solve problems.
>
> (the Home of Migrants College, 28 November 2012)

The outward development aimed to combine one's personal development with collective interests to enhance their cooperative ability. A picture, used to illustrate the report, described two teams of participants in this college (see Figure 6.1). Conducted by a team leader waving a banner, each team was supposed to walk in locked step, all the team members being bound on two long squared timbers by feet. The one who reached the finish line was the winner. This game called for close cooperation amid the participants to move on. Similar extracurricular activities were required of each class.

Figure 6.1 Outward Development organized by the Home of Migrants College, 2012. Selected from the College website

Outward development and assemblage of new rules and events

I observed how the students of two classes, whom I taught English, planned and implemented their outward development projects. As this practice was a coherent part of the total curriculum, the students and the class mentors were required to put it on schedule. The Machinery Engineering Class had been negotiating their plan over the early half of 2013 but could not reach an agreement. Later I learned that they managed to organize some group activity after I left my fieldwork.

However, I participated in an outdoor activity held by the Class of Economic Management. The students in the Class of Economic Management started to discuss their extracurricular plan. They finally decided to pay a tourism company for an outward development, which was, as would be explained by the trainer from this company on the day that the activity took place, 'to use outdoor activities to develop people's potential and promote people's cooperative ability'. (Fieldwork notes, 12 May 2013)

To put the ideas into practice, both the student representatives and class mentor, Zhao Daming, called on all the students to participate in this activity. Many students joined online discussion. This event finally became a reality in the middle of May 2013 after two months' negotiation (see Figure 6.2). Around 7:30 that morning, we were ready to set off. Only 20 participants, including class mentor Zhao Daming, 14 students, and 4 friends or children of some students, far less than I had expected, as there were over 140 students in this class. Most of us present were class representatives. Half were employees of a bus company including Meili and Lingling, as mentioned in Chapter 3. It seemed that only a small number of people were enthusiastic about this activity.

Soon, the trainer, known to us as Mr. Huang, turned up. He brought along two minibuses, one of which was driven by the trainer himself, so he played multiple roles: a trainer, a driver and a tour guide. The other bus was driven by a professional driver, supposedly hired by Mr. Huang. We each paid 160 Yuan and collected it and hand it over to the trainer. The trainer gave

Figure 6.2 An outward development project with students of the Home of Migrants College, 2012. Taken by the author of this book

a formal introduction to the definition of 'outward development' as well as today's general plan. Then we took a group picture in the foyer of the Home of Migrants College with the class flag, which bore the class slogan: 'Coming for dreams and gathered because of miracle', as quoted in Chapter 3.

> When arriving at Peng Village, the first destination, Mr. Huang told us general instructions about how to complete game tasks and divided us into three groups: blue, red and yellow, according to the colours of the uniforms we had been assigned. Briefly speaking, we would complete some tasks, through which a clear understanding of this village would be achieved. Mr. Huang directed us to do some warming up exercises like stretching legs and arms, saying this would protect us from getting hurt. I happened to be in the same yellow group with five students and three children of some students. We selected Dawei as our group leader, who was a driver from the bus company...
>
> Nearly 12:30 pm, at the planned gathering point, we group members all went to the scheduled place, but no other groups had turned up there except the trainer himself. So, we went scattered again to see more of the scenic spots, which had been neglected as we had been focused on the assigned tasks. The other two groups did not take this task very seriously and had fun...
>
> The lunch was arranged in a restaurant, where food was enough to satisfy hunger. 'We cannot expect more as the total price is 160 yuan for the whole day', one student explained to me as if it were his fault. After the lunch, seaside riding was arranged and then we were divided into groups again and played soldiers.
>
> (Fieldwork notes, 12 May 2013)

In the rest of this chapter, I will explore the implications from this activity by adopting the concept of development as discourse and the Deleuzian concept of assemblage. Escobar (2007) highlights how local knowledge can be produced in relation to development interventions either adopting the way of 'the adaptation, subversions and resistance' or taking 'the alternative strategies' (21). By taking this insight as a lens, I analyse how students responded to the development discourses from school administration, enterprise management and student representatives to examine the tensions between what was advocated and what was implemented. From the perspective of assemblage,

I gained the understanding that the outward development project brought the Yuanmeng students into a neighbouring area through a commercial move, where rules and events were prescribed by a commercial institution.

University life: From collective to de-institutionalized

There seemed to be a contradiction between what adult learning for university education should be and what it was. Both the students and the staff suggested that the university education they were having was not the same as full-time university education. To create a university atmosphere, the students were encouraged to conduct collective activities such as outward development.

As indicated above, when planning this outward development project, the students in the Class of Economic Management did not show enough interest in it. To encourage more people to participate, class mentor Zhao Daming put forward the following notice in their QQ chatroom:

> Dear students,
> It will be a rare opportunity for us to have a collective activity. I hope all of us will participate in it. As many of us are not familiar with each other and our friendship is not deep enough, we need a platform for more communication. To learn here is more than work for a certificate but to make this process as colourful and diverse as university life. This would give us a feeling for university. This will be real 'Yuanmeng'.
> (Class Mentor's notice in QQ chatroom, 05 May 2013)

To re-echo the mentor's notice, Zhao Rong, class representative, called on her classmates in the QQ chatroom: 'This is a rare new journey and a good opportunity to be acquainted with new classmates and make new friends. Do not miss it!' (QQ chatroom notes, 05 May 2013). Zhao Rong's remark is understandable, as she was supposed to coordinate between the college administration and the students.

Zhao Daming used 'as colourful and diverse as university life' and 'a feeling for university', which indicates that he felt where they were studying was not 'real' university. Students like Zhao Rong believed collective activity was a fundamental aspect of 'real' university life. The fluttering class flag and the class slogan on it, described above, suggest that some students, especially class representatives, cherished their common university dream and called for class cohesion. Subsequently, they attempted to transform their learning and teaching into 'real university' by adopting collective study and activity, as the 'outward development' herein discussed.

The requirement for collective activities in the Home of Migrants College can be further demonstrated in my interview with Wang Shaogang, Vice President: 'The positionality of our college is the combination of individual interests and the collective interests. The driving force of the city propels the development of the state. To realize this, changes are the fundamental force. Migrant workers must be disciplined and trained to enter a civilian society' (Interview notes, 21 October 2012). As stated earlier in this chapter, the practice of 'outward development' was a coherent part of the total curriculum in this college and it seems to suggest that university life meant collective community. Delivering lectures in the classroom to students was one of the measures to achieve this effect, again as Wang Shaogang said: 'Different from some other correspondence schools, our college provides weekends teaching for students, as they need environment, a place where they can learn to be sociable and cooperate in a teamwork with their classmates. This is something that ordinary correspondence schools such as online teaching cannot achieve' (Interview notes, 21 October 2012).

Here, Wang Shaogang explained the advantages and features of the Home of Migrants College in running its adult education programmes in that collective environment and face-to-face teaching were provided. However, to have a collective extracurricular activity with high attendance rate was not easy to realize as the students were scattered in different enterprises and living quarters. This was shown in the low attendance in this outward development. So it appeared that there existed a tension between what adult university education was like and what it should be like.

The students were influenced by discourses from the college staff and documents enhancing intervention activities. The college administration as well as some students such as class representatives and leaders seemed to hold that collective activity such as extracurricular work was an important part of their university life. Therefore, the college authorities and the students' mentor encouraged their students to participate in the outward development project.

The class representatives, as the student leaders, also assisted in promoting this activity. However, some students could, to use the words of Escobar (2007), adopt 'the adaptation, subversions and resistance', or take 'the alternative strategies' (21) when encountering relevant intervention projects. They did not seem to support the idea that collective activities were necessary for their university education. They chose to avoid these activities.

Then there appeared the tension between controlling and escaping from being controlled in education management. The college administration needed more opportunities to exert their existence. This could be achieved in a collective environment. However, this sense of authority was being challenged by the fact that some students, due to various reasons, had difficulties or unwillingness to participate in collective activities. In the case of this outward development, most of them did not show up at all. I will analyse different discourses around why this happened.

Absenteeism for different social actors

The low attendance rate in the outward development project had already been anticipated in the middle of its planning. This seemed to be disappointing to some student representatives. One of them spoke in the class QQ chatroom: 'As some of us do not cherish friendship, we will anyway go ahead with this programme' (QQ chat, 08 May 2013). This suggests that one could be labelled with 'not cherishing friendship' if not engaged in this activity.

However, there were different voices for why they would be absent when encountering relevant intervention projects. Sometime after this activity, I gained a different understanding why not many students had participated in this activity. Zhao Daming, class mentor, told me that class activities, such as outward development, were not required for the assessment of students. Some of them would rather 'have a day off work' than join this programme, as a student, one of the youngest in the Class of Economic Management, admitted in the class QQ chatroom. Consequently, uninformed absenteeism was employed as an option to escape from social activity and social power, but they did not inform whether they would attend the event but simply did not turn up. If they could not evade it, they would delay making the decision, as in the case of the Class of Machinery Engineering. So the students were free to choose to be absent, as it was not a required part of the curriculum.

This activity then served as a social platform which brought the students together and strengthened their relationship, as Zhao Daming, class mentor, emphasized above, 'our friendship is not deep enough, we thus need a platform for more communication'. The students offered diverse responses to the design and implementation of this activity. There existed a tension between those who promoted the outward development project and those who passively resisted it. This indicates that collective activities which were intended to strengthen friendship and collectivism, if not a required part of the college curriculum, appeared to give way to other individual considerations like jobs, rest and hobbies.

When development was a commercial activity

It appeared that money played a vital role in putting the design of this outward development to reality, as the students paid for it and a trainer was paid to organize it. Thus, throughout the practice ran a power struggle between commercialism and collectivism. This training of development was fundamentally a commercial activity, as it was undertaken by a tourism company. So it would be likely to lead to similar results coming from any other commercial activity. There was naturally a negotiation process between a tourism company and class representatives.

Later during the training, as described above, some of the trainer's course designs became a symbolical act, such as doing warming up exercises and offering test papers, which created a serious and formal atmosphere. In addition, some of his promises and pre-arrangements were not able to be fulfilled. For instance, he finally did not announce the answers to the questions in the test or make any comments. This meant that the development programme was not engaging or challenging enough for adult learners, thus it seemed to be no more than a child's play. Jiangang, the oldest student and a bus driver, who was over forty, commented partially jokingly at the end of this whole day: 'Today's development programme has been indeed watered down (*shui* 水)'. By this, he meant the programmes were not so rich as expected.

Also, some students were not satisfied with the food, 'which was enough to satisfy one's hunger', as mentioned in the fieldnotes above, because the trainer needed to take every care not to exceed his budget while he was not genuinely controlling the participants, who had paid him. It was related to the commercialization that dominated this relationship involving relevant people. The practice of the trainer reflects the permeation of commercialism in the Yuanmeng plans, such as their student recruitment campaigns, as introduced in Chapter 3.

While college curriculum was promoting collective extracurricular activities like the outward development, it did not stipulate it as a part of assessment or provide financial support for it. Thereby, commercialization of this activity was inevitable. In other words, the commercialization gradually gained power over the promotion for collective activities. The college authorities intended to exert more influence on their students by encouraging collective extracurricular activities, but they did not provide funding for this plan. The students had the right to pay or not to pay, or to join or to dodge it. It appears that, in this negotiating process, it was the commercialism that loosened the students from collectivism.

Tensions between collectivism and commercialism

Tensions and contradictions between collectivism and commercialism provided opportunities for personal development, which was encouraged to be combined with collective interests. Within the competing discourses around development, such as outward development, personal development and collective interests, existed the relationship between normalizing authorities and escaping individuals. This relationship embodied multiple aspects of the learning and life of adult learners. This finding could be linked with the observation made by UNESCO (2020) in the context of 'a continuous learning ethos pervading all spheres of life': 'Lifelong learning has deeply changed how the "typical" life course is perceived and how people deal with its complexities' (12).

The Home of Migrants College was interested in organizing activities to unite their members. As the outward development activity was an optional part of curriculum and financed by participants themselves, it was hard to make a rigid requirement that all join this programme. The college authorities were not willing to give up their ideals for the norms of university life and practice. The student representatives and the class mentor prompted the students to be engaged in this activity by arousing their sense of collectivism and friendship, but this strategy did not seem to be working effectively, as evidenced from the students' responses. Some students did not resist openly the development programme but chose to keep silent, as in the case of the Economic Management Class herein discussed. Others kept delaying their decision, as in the case of the Machinery Engineering Class, as mentioned above.

The class mentor and the student representatives contracted this outward development project to a commercial institution. Thereby, they were extended into a new assemblage, where new rules, people and resources were brought together and where the rules on the project were prescribed by the commercial institution. Consequently, they were joined by new forces of commercialization. The ideology of collectivism was being challenged by commercialization and individualism, as has been revealed in such educational procedures as student recruitment and 'interactive teaching' in the previous chapters and will be further discussed in the next chapter.

7

Examining Assessment of Students

When assessment is a central concern

In exploring assessment of students in the education of migrant workers in Yuanda Province, especially in combination with my experiences as a temporary teacher of English in the Home of Migrants College, I came to understand that assessment, as a process, could be more interactive than the phase of teaching and learning.

Bourdieu and Passeron (1990) describe how examinations triggered worries and motivations for students: 'Commentators have often enough described the anxiety engendered by the total, harsh and partly unpredictable verdicts of the traditional tests, or the dislocated rhythm inherent in a system of organizing schoolwork which, in its most anomic forms, tends to acknowledge no other incentive than the imminence of an absolute deadline' (142). Similar responses and atmosphere could be perceived in the Home of Migrants College. The word that I heard most frequently as a researcher and a teacher of English was 'examination'. This indicated that assessment, although seemingly the final stage of teaching and learning, had been a consistent concern for both the teachers and the students, as illustrated by the teaching practice of Liang Meijing, as described in Chapter 5.

In this chapter, I will further explore the teaching and administration in the migrant workers' education in Yuanda Province but focus on how assessment was planned and conducted. I will examine the assessment as a dynamic process to see how assessment principles and contents were stipulated and completed, and what complex relations were involved within this process.

The previous chapter drew mainly on the data from my observations of three teachers. This chapter builds on the ideas mainly from my own teaching experiences in the Home of Migrants College. I will make an occasional comparison with the assessment practice in the Yuanda Yuanmeng Plan. My experiences as a teacher in the Home of Migrants College helped me gain in-depth understanding of how the assessment was completed.

The concept of hidden curriculum provides a resource to explore the tension between what had been planned in curriculum and what was implemented. On this basis, with the concept of Deleuzian assemblage as a lens, I see assessment of students as a dynamic process, which involved relationships between rules, resources, events, education workers and students, and power (Kabeer 1994). In addition, I will bring in the ideas of Bourdieu and Passeron (1990) on the relationship between examinations and social reproduction to investigate the examinations in the Yuanmeng plans.

Handwritten references for open book examinations

As stated in Chapter 5, I had a group meeting with a few key figures of administration and teaching to ensure my teaching quality in the Home of Migrants College. I also received a written notice titled 'Supplementary rules for teaching administration of Yuanmeng Plan academic degree courses' ('Supplementary rules'). One of the rules stressed the importance of handwritten assignments: 'for every subject, students should give handwritten assignments, which should be submitted to class representatives before the next class sessions'; in other words, printed assignments and the e-copies would not be accepted. This way, as Zhou Li, who oversaw online teaching affairs, suggested, was 'just intended to let them learn a bit more'.

Likewise, for most of the subjects, 'open book exams' were offered as a way of assessment. The students were allowed to refer to any handwritten material as well as their textbooks. Wang Shaogang, Vice President of this college, elaborated on his understanding of 'open book exams' with handwritten references:

> Of knowledge and behaviour norm, I think the latter is more important. It is important to promote their quality. To realise this, we conduct flexible

examinations and assessments. It is designed to combine general studies with their work. Examinees are not supposed to take printed and photocopied materials with them but take handwritten materials with them. Firstly, the preparing process is itself a process of writing, memorising and reviewing. Secondly, even if the examinees take references with themselves, they will have no time to use the materials if they are not well prepared.

(Interview notes, 21 October 2012)

Wang Shaogang seemed to believe that by preparing handwritten material for examinations, the students would be able to devote more time and energy to their learning process, and this served as a method ensuring the students appropriate engagement in their learning. Thereby, he used the assessment to discipline and stimulate students. He thought it was more important to cultivate students' behaviour than to evaluate how much they had learned by means of assessment.

However, the college administration's insistence on handwritten materials triggered controversy over what was to be handwritten, and what material to be printed or photocopied among the students in the Economic Management Class and the Machinery Engineering Class. The argument was concerned with their textbooks of English uploaded by Beijing Skyline University, their degree-awarding institution. These books each consisted of four units, with each unit having lists of words and phrases, dialogues, texts and exercises, all the units being related to either economy or technology, depending on their majors. However, the textbooks were of e-forms in their virtual classrooms instead of printed ones. Then there arose a disagreement on what was a textbook and what were printed references. The college authorities and the students negotiated for a couple of months. Then class representative Zhao Rong announced in their virtual chatroom: 'The printed texts as well as words and phrases lists can be brought into testing rooms, but the texts should not contain their Chinese translations. The printed exercises after the texts cannot be brought into testing rooms. In a word, all handwritten materials can be carried. All the above notice is subject to the explanation of the college authorities' (Class virtual chatroom record, 04 June 2013).

The Home of Migrants College administration and teaching staff attempted to engage students in learning. However, they were at a loss for how to conduct the rule on 'handwritten materials' with the increasing impact of digital technology. It seemed to be paradoxical that not all learning materials from downloaded English textbooks were allowed into test rooms. As a result, some students copied down more than what was needed. So, as one of their daily greetings, the students often exchanged information with each other in their virtual chatrooms about how much they had copied for the examinations. Evidently, the assessment of students involved experiences of 'anxiety' and 'incentive' (Bourdieu and Passeron 1990: 142).

The college authorities seemed to be afraid to lose control over their students when there was easy access to the internet and virtual learning resources. They insisted on the rule that students bring in handwritten reference materials for open book examinations. Meanwhile, they were undecided over the definition of 'textbook'. To regain control over learning resources, they changed their definition of 'textbook'; in other words, they modified the rule that the students utilize their learning resources. As a result, the students needed to copy manually more reference material than they otherwise would. The college acted as an education provider and assessor; thereby, it used its power to adjust the rule of assessment to elevate its level of difficulties. Thus, the assessment of students participating in adult education was a dynamic negotiation, as it took into consideration examinees' situations and partnership institutions. This education process involved social relationships and ideological conflicts, as discussed below.

Mock test designs: Intention and outcome

Rule 2 in 'Supplementary rules', as stated earlier in this chapter, required that students draft up test papers. This intended the students to be deeply involved in teaching and learning process. This assignment could be completed in collaboration with a few other students either by handwriting or on a computer. This measure newly introduced by the college, according to Zhou Li, coordinator of online administration and teaching, was 'to let students have more practice in their subjects' to 'strengthen their teamwork spirit'. Chen Yi, responsible for adult education, stressed that 'It is a new strategy. We are trying to push students to learn something, to participate and be engaged in teaching and learning. In a word, they can learn something from each other both after class and in class' (Group meeting notes, 26 February 2013).

I had thought that students would accept this assignment without any query. However, they reacted to this new rule in drastically different ways. Some were very careful while others challenged and changed it. These can be examined with Escobar's (2007) idea as a lens to investigate how 'local people' use 'the adaptation, subversions and resistance' to react to 'development interventions' (21).

To encourage students to be fully engaged, I promised that I would select test questions from the collection of papers designed by them and use the questions in their final tests. One day in the middle of April 2013, morning sessions were given to the Class of Economic Management and afternoon sessions transferred to the Class of Machinery Engineering. The teaching process was just like any other day of teaching. However, when it came to the assignment of drafting up test papers as a new measure, there arose some noise and even arguments:

> Meili, one of the oldest students in the Class of Economic Management, remarked: 'So we are just guinea pigs'. I said: 'Each student just will do a bit. You can work together. Every few students form a group, and you can design a set of test paper together. This will not be much, so you will not use a lot of time. Anyway, this is the decision from the administration from our college or from Beijing Skyline University, which I am not so sure. Why not try it?' The students did not give any further responses.
>
> (Fieldwork notes, 14 April 2013)

Meili used 'guinea pigs' to challenge the rule for this assignment. No one else raised any further questions. The students were supposed to submit this assignment sometime around the middle of May 2013. But the queries raised by Meili show that adult students had their own independent minds on how their education should be implemented. The afternoon sessions for the Class of Machinery Engineering were more eventful than the morning sessions, as shown below:

> Liu Qiang, a student from Sichuan Province, was as impulsive as ever. He said: 'You should not let us students draft test papers, as this will definitely

give more burden to us'. I tried to explain the meaning of this assignment, but he could not control his anger. So finally, I added: 'I am just announcing the decision from our college'. He said, 'You are now working for this college, and will certainly defend for them'. I was at a loss for what to say. After a moment of silence, he added: 'I cannot bear it'.

(Fieldwork notes 14 April 2013)

As one of the key informants, Liu Qiang was a distinctive character, strong-willed and fiery tempered. Liu Qiang differentiated 'you' from 'us', as in 'You should not let us students draft test papers, as this will definitely give more burden to us'. I was surprised that Liu Qiang did not see this assignment as a learning opportunity but as a piece of work supposedly assumed by the teacher. I was equally surprised that he should put me on the same side with the college authorities. But I realized that this was my own problem: I had not fully identified myself with being a teacher and an insider but situated myself more as an outsider and as a researcher. But what the students were concerned about was not whether I was an outside researcher but who taught them and how they would be assessed.

The test papers had been scheduled to be submitted sometime around the middle of May. Some of them did it even earlier than that. One of the most impressive groups was from a sub-teaching site, which means I never met them in person. They posted to me their tests papers with each of them designing a complete set of test paper by handwriting rather than each contributing a part towards a set of test paper. That must have involved a large amount of work, though this was not based on students' collaboration to strengthen their teamwork spirit.

Spontaneous responses from such students as Liu Qiang and Meili suggested that there existed misunderstandings or even conflicts between teachers and students, as the students thought that designing assessment was an extra burden supposed to be assumed by the teachers. As stated by Grillo (1997), there tends to be 'a significant distance between ideas and practices of development agencies and those of "local" people' (25). Various responses to this assignment, as described above, demonstrated competing values and practices from the students. The teachers had meant designing test papers to be a learning opportunity while enhancing the cooperative ability of the students. However, for the students, designing tests papers was not a form of practice and learning but a responsibility to be taken by the teaching staff. This showed the students began to bring into the educational field their sense of their own right and obligations, which were mainly formulated in the commercial society and enterprise culture.

In addition, the rule that designing test papers was required of students indicated the internal anxiety of the college administration about examinations. This might, in turn, have increased students' anxiety about their examinations. This further demonstrated that the central position that assessment occupied in the college activities, as has been discussed in Chapter 5 on the teaching process.

Thirdly, some students did not conduct this assignment on a collaborative basis but on an individual basis. This was not what the curriculum planner had intended. The discrepancy between curriculum design and curriculum practice made me realize that, as the students were mainly engaged in a blended form of learning and offline learning, they were faced with varied difficulties, as discussed in Chapter 5, such as insufficient assessment mechanisms (Adedoyin and Soykan 2020; Vlachopoulos 2020), incompetent digital technologies and inadequate access to online resources (Adedoyin and Soykan 2020). This might have reduced their opportunities to discuss and complete their collaborative assignment, thereby impacting their motivation to conduct a group work project. This suggested the importance that the instructor should administer learning and assessment tasks appropriately designed for adult learners.

In short, this section explored how migrant workers understood, adapted and implemented the practice of drafting the mock test paper. It examined the discrepancies between the rule of drafting test papers and its actual practices, demonstrating the migrants exhibited strong commercial sense and awareness of their own rights, as some of them attempted to understand the education practice from a commercial perspective.

Assessment as an interactive social process

Assessment in my experience in the Home of Migrants College was a lengthy process involving supervising universities, college's administration, teaching and students' responses. As I was not familiar with the general practice of this college, I needed to make constant adjustments to the demands of the college and the specific conditions of the students.

I was motivated to explore the implications within these relationships with Deleuze's concept of assemblage as a lens. I was aware that Deleuzian assemblage stresses multiplicity of entities in interaction both corporeal and incorporeal; however, I focus on examining the combinations amid the dimensions such as resources, rules, people, events and power in the approach of the Social Relations Framework (Kabeer 1994), as I did in the previous chapters. Meanwhile, an assemblage of heterogeneous factors connects other assemblages, showing multiplicities of planes of relationships.

When interviewing Wang Shaogang, Vice President, I learned that the assessment involved multiple interacting parties. When I asked if the other relevant authorities or the relevant universities allowed his college to administer assessment to students, Wang Shaogang replied succinctly: 'That is our condition. If they do not give us the permission, we would not cooperate with them' (Interview notes, 21 October 2012).

The idea of power and its implications can mirror how the Home of Migrants College established partnerships with different institutions. Kabeer (1994) argues: 'power is constituted as an integral feature of institutional life through its norms, its distribution of resources and responsibilities and its practice' (282). This suggests that power can be combined with such heterogeneous dimensions as rules, resources and events, in that power exists in discourses and rules, resources production and allocation and all the activities. In a similar vein, as the Home of Migrants College acted as the agent for migrant workers' training and was able to allocate funding resources, this college had the power to decide whom to collaborate with.

The Home of Migrants College negotiated with partnership institutions and gained the power to assess its students, thus expanding its academic and social impact. This can be linked with the idea of Kabeer (1994): institutions are subject to change 'by the practice of different institutional actors through processes of bargaining and negotiation' (283). The power to assess students in the Home of Migrants College served as the precondition to cooperate with relevant course supervisors and degree awarders. These institutions, however, played a guiding role in the policy design and implementation of assessment of students. For instance, I learned from my teaching experiences that Beijing

Skyline University stipulated that the students of the Economic Management Class and the Machinery Engineering Class have an adequate record of their online learning time and complete some online assignments before they were qualified to take the tests given by the Home of Migrants College.

In addition, to be adapted to the impact from multiple stakeholders, I was sliding and floating onto different assemblages of factors such as rules and discourses, affectivity, power and social actors. I was supervised by a degree-awarding institution, Beijing Skyline University. What is more noteworthy, I was in close contact with the students and the staff in the Home of Migrants College. This intimate relationship can embody the Deleuzian assemblage as 'a symbiosis, a "sympathy"' (Deleuze and Parnet 1987: 69), which suggests the affectivity of human elements. Deleuze and Guattari (1994) explain later in a different context that affects are not affections but can transcend 'the strength of those who undergo them' (1994: 164). Thus, affects are pre-individual and independent of individual human beings. I felt the impact of affectivity from my relationships with the social actors I had direct contact with, especially with the migrant students.

In face-to-face communication, most of the students, especially the younger ones, were silent about what I should do with the final test designing and strategies. Some older and talkative students like Meili, a coordinator in a bus company, and Jiangang, a bus driver in the same company and in his mid-forties, would have a chat with me. We even had a day out for 'the outward development', as discussed in Chapter 6. This deepened our mutual understanding and friendship. This was also an occasion on which students could express their suggestions or lobby me 'informally' on how and what was to be tested. As Meili said of Jiangang, 'Sir, he is old and pathetic. He does not have a command of much English. Let him pass the test. We are no longer young here. The younger ones have no such difficulties as us'. Jiangang also admitted: 'I have not learned much of English. You see my son is going to take university entrance exams this year, but I am still here learning'. This exerted some pressure on my assessment plans, as students like Jiangang were hard-working and they would attend the class and take notes very carefully.

By contrast, students' online chat was much more challenging than face-to-face communication. The students in their QQ chatrooms, as usual, would have a heated discussion about anything including exams. Sometimes, I was involved in the discussion. They expressed their concerns and put forward some suggestions. As the following QQ chat indicated:

> A: Sir, can you just focus your exam contents on the textbook and be sure not to exceed the textbook?
> B: Then give more multiple choices for the exam paper.
> Me: We would stick to our textbook.
> C: I just feel at a loss for where to start for the review.
> D: Sir, try to make test questions simpler.
> B: Then we just recite and write down 26 alphabetical letters? (emoji of laughter)
> C: Yea, Yea, all of us agree that the test questions should be simpler.
> E: Yes, absolutely.
> A: Be sure not to make test questions flexible and changeable. The contents in the textbook are more than we can digest.
> F: I think the difficulty level in our entrance exams is just good.
> G: Yea, Yea. Make it simple one, sir.
> H: Design more multiple choices.
> I: Yes, otherwise, all of us will fail.
> E: Please, sir, let us pass. We will be well impressed with you and be grateful to you.
> D: Teacher of Management Studies, will you also have pity on us? We students have difficulties. We lead a hard life as migrant workers, and the students are located at the lowest level of society.
> (the Economic Management Class QQ chat record, 08 May 2013)

I realized there were some elements of joking in such requests as 'reciting 26 alphabetical letters', 'have pity on us' and 'Let us pass. We will be well impressed with you and be grateful to you'. These requests were able to be expressed more freely in virtual spaces than in face-to-face communication, which, consequently, strengthened the influence of affectivity.

Wang Shaogang seemed to have anticipated these situations and comments. In his online article, he commented upon students' university entrance exams: while acknowledging that 'the majority of students' treated exams in a positive attitude, he stated:

> The minority of migrant workers had not done any preparatory work before taking exams; as a result, they became a Mr. Zero by submitting a blank paper.

Some others even went further than that. They simply ignored invigilator's requirements and testing room disciplines. When their misbehaviour was found out, some tore apart their test papers, some were grudging and others complained about the difficulties of exam questions.

(the Home of Migrants College report, collected on 03 December 2012)

It could be a consistent trend that some students expected tests to be easier. They seemed to assume that they were being reasonable in doing so. However, the college authorities like Wang Shaogang pointed out that students needed to work harder:

Some migrant workers do not take hard working attitude towards their learning or have real senior middle school literacy foundation... 68 per cent of the new generation migrant workers take rest, surfing online, shopping, watching TV or working for extra money as their first choice for their spare time. This means that some new generation migrant workers have not established awareness of capital investment. Although they have development goals, they have not devoted time, energy and money to overcome their difficulties, thus abandoning opportunities for further development.

(the Home of Migrants College report, collected on 03 December 2012)

Wang Shaogang, from the perspective of the college authorities, argued that nearly two thirds of migrant workers chose something other than learning as their first spare time activity, thus they needed to work harder. Somewhat different from Wang Shaogang's resiliency, I found myself facing pressure from the college administration, as it contacted constantly either by online messenger or phone call about my progress of teaching and assessing. The group meeting, as mentioned above, designated the general guidelines to observe in the assessment implementation. Therein, I was told to consider how to assess students in the way that a proper percentage of them passing final examinations, or as Xiao Zhiyuan, my gatekeeper, said around 70 to 80 per cent of them. This meant that I should take into consideration students' learning abilities and progress before I designed test papers and testing standards; actually, as Zhou Li said in our group meeting, 'Some students are poor in English. They may be like senior middle school students or even junior middle school students'.

Under the influence of different requirements and the general atmosphere in this college, I began to consider how to ensure around 80 per cent of the students pass the tests while ensuring the fairness of assessment. In this process, I tended to forget my role as a researcher and why I came to join in this education programme, but I felt the impact of affectivity and seemed to have entered the state of pure affect, where I had the same concerns as other social actors. For instance, some students were older like Jiangang mentioned above, and they needed more effort to pass English. Others lived far away from the teaching site. They could spend three or four hours on the way to school and back home for weekend sessions.

Even if I had been cautious with the test design, things were not satisfactory for the administrators of the Home of Migrants College. After I submitted my designed test papers, Chen Yi contacted me more often than other administrators when assessments were drawing nearer and discussed with me any assessment difficulties and test paper contents in relation to students' learning levels. She thought the test papers were 'a bit too much in question numbers and too hard for the students at this level. Of course, this would be rather easy for you, but for students it could be hard', as Chen Yi told me in a roundabout way over a phone call. The request of the students that their tests be 'easier', as a discourse, seemed to have impacted Chen Yi and other administrators. Accordingly, I made changes in the test papers, including three sets of papers for each class at the same time. Chen Yi was right, as indeed a percentage of them still failed in the test, which sounded like a reasonable result. Otherwise, there would be too many failing cases if they had used the papers which I had designed for the first time.

Analysing reactions from different social actors in the case of the Home of Migrants College showed that the assessment process of adult education involved constant negotiation among multiple parties such as administrators from degree-awarding institutions, course-providing college, teaching staff and students. Bourdieu and Passeron (1990) draw us to 'the illusion of the neutrality and independence of the school system with respect to the structure of class relations' (141). This suggests that the examinations conducted in the Home of Migrants College, as a social practice, constructed power rather than being neutral. In addition, the examinations were involved in social relations.

To balance power and benefit distribution among different stakeholders, social actors relevant to the examinations negotiated and interacted with each other in completing the procedure of the assessment of students. In this process, the strategies typically employed in commercial bargaining were adopted. Also, official discourses such as documents, rules and leaders' speeches displayed the resilient aspects in running the Haibin Yuanmeng Plan.

However, practical concerns from students, teachers and administrators exhibited flexible discourses. This exerted influences on how assessment polices should be changed and adjusted to the levels of the students. The contradiction between the hegemony of official discourses and the resistance from the lower levels such as the students' voices was reflected in the process of assessment of students from their policy making, test papers' design, test paper approval and changes and test paper marking.

Finally, in the process of assessment, the teachers' role seemed to have been reduced. This could be linked to the remark of Kelly (2009) on assessment, according to which, the assessment practice, contextualized in the British school system, has been used in 'direct political control', 'combating that centrality of the teacher', and 'imposing a narrow and bureaucratic form of teacher accountability' (18). As in my case, I had to modify test papers a few times to be adapted to the requirements and situations involving a few parties. In addition, even as a teacher and an assessor, I did not know exactly the results of the students' assessment, as my marking would be integrated with other factors such as students' attendance rates, online learning results and online test results. As a result, the role of the teacher had been reduced to one of the links in the assessment process.

Some authorities such as Wang Shaogang believed, as cited above, nearly two-thirds of the migrant workers chose anything other than learning as their first spare time activity. Therefore, the students needed to work harder. On the other hand, the students complained they needed more help as their abilities were inadequate for learning. I was interested in discovering why such a controversy arose. If students had low-learning capacities, they did not ask how to learn better but only considered how to pass examinations with more ease by having the criteria for examinations lowered. This could be linked to what students as well as general society thought about the value of adult degree education, as discussed below.

'Don't require the same of us as you would of full-time students'

As discussed above, education administrators, instructors and students were all involved in the final implementation of examinations. In this process, some students asked the instructors to design easier test questions. Their inward motivation to raise this request could be linked to what they thought about the education programme they were engaged in.

So, in designing examination questions, I found myself in a constant state of adjustment. For each class, teaching for a few days was allocated across a semester. This meant that I should consider how to combine teaching with the evaluation of the students from the very beginning. In the second meeting with the students, I told them of my proposed plan for final tests, which would include translation of words and phrases between English and Chinese, paragraph translations, writing sentences and paragraphs, as well as the most used form of multiple choices, for I was told the exams would be in the form of 'open-book exams'. The students could bring any references, all of which, except their printed textbooks, should be handwritten. This had been informed even at the very first meeting when I interviewed Wang Shaogang.

When the Class of Machinery Engineering heard this, Liu Qiang shouted immediately: 'That is too difficult for us. You cannot expect too highly of us, as we are not full-time students. The requirements of them do not apply to us' (Classroom observation notes, 14 April 2013). Later on the same day with the Economic Management Class, similar things happened:

> A female student complained when she heard my explanation about my plan for the final test: 'You cannot require of us the same as you do full time university students'. I asked: 'Why not? We should keep up our image. The Yuanmeng Plan has been in existence for many years'. This lady immediately stopped, but I did not think she was convinced.
>
> (Fieldwork notes, 14 April 2013)

When I said this, I found myself acting as an insider of the Home of Migrants College, a staff member, as I attempted to use the social influence of 'Yuanmeng Plan' as evidence to inspire them. My remark was imposing in the discourse of the college authorities that this student felt lost for how to reply. Interestingly, the students insisted that they were different from full time university students, thus they felt they had reason to be treated and assessed by different criteria.

The general opinion about adult education students and fulltime students who were recruited through rigid general university entrance exams was indeed that the former was inferior to the latter. As Wang Shaogang also admitted, 'One's academic certificate may show one has improved in ability, anyway. Those who have obtained the certificates from us, which may not be the first-class ones, but are recognized and accredited by the state, have the chances to be promoted. But I don't think certificate is the most important' (Interview notes 21 October 2012).

Wang Shaogang, as a representative of the Haibin Yuanmeng Plan, had attempted to speak for the importance of migrant workers' education programme. He mentioned 'academic certificate', 'ability', 'recognised and accredited by the state' and 'not most important'. The quick switches in his narration betrayed uncertainties and contradictions in his attitudes towards education and development. The key in this quotation was 'recognized by the state', which was, however, not an expression for high commendation, as it showed the actual situation that adult education certificates were merely recognised by the state, providing chances for people's promotion. To distract from the focus on the inferiority of the adult education certification, Wang added that certificate was not 'the most important'.

Relevant point-based regulations on joining Haibin household registration system were also telling. The students I taught would be able to claim sixty points after they acquired the certificate while full-time counterparts would be able to claim another ten more points. While the general society tended to take adult education certificates as merely 'acknowledged and accredited by the state', it was still surprising to see that adult students themselves like those in the Home of Migrants College felt the same.

Students' pessimistic expectation of their examinations reflected their sense of low self-esteem and identity crisis, as they were not confident if they were 'real' university students. They expected to have their examinations simplified. This could be one of the reasons why they did not want to work hard to obtain the graduation certificate. This sense of uncertainty has been reflected and discussed in Chapter 6 when the students' 'outward development' activity was examined and will be further discussed in Chapter 8.

Power, affect and commercialization

In this chapter, I examined the practice of the assessment in the Home of Migrants College as a process. This process integrated multiple and dynamic relationships including supervising institutions, college authorities, teachers and students. The wide range of partnerships established by the Home of Migrants College produced influential educational events and consolidated the material status of the Home of Migrants College.

In conducting the assessment, I had close contact and conversations with some staff and students of the Home of Migrants College, enabling me to gain a deep understanding of their concerns within the system of the assessment. This inspired my sympathy with them, which transcended language and rational thinking. Thereby, affect was liberated out of the individuated feelings towards a 'a zone of indetermination, of indiscernibility, as if things, beasts, and persons... endlessly reach that point that immediately precedes their natural differentiation' (Deleuze and Guattari 1994: 173). This impact of affectivity was not based on logic but on eliciting impersonal and preverbal affect, shared by all social actors involved.

What is noteworthy, commercialization was revealed in power negotiation and distribution in the assessment process. As analysed earlier, test implementation engaged different educational stakeholders. This can be linked with the research studies on the influence of examinations. For instance, Lowe (1999) furnishes an illuminating analysis of how international examination systems have become a part of a commercialization process by 'serving global capitalism through the certification of human resources for a global market' and argues that the qualifications are both 'a product and a form of currency in other parts of the market' (329). This suggests that testing services can construct power and contribute to the economic and cultural development. As shown in the assessment practices in the Home of Migrants College, negotiation and bargaining, which were usually employed in the activities of commercial bargaining, had been adopted in designing and implementing the assessment of students.

The idea of Bourdieu and Passeron (1990: 141), as stated earlier in this chapter, enabled me to understand that there would be no absolute neutrality or justice in conducting the examination. In addition, the examination can 'inspire universal recognition of the legitimacy of academic verdicts and of the social hierarchies they legitimate' (ibid, 162), thereby validating and consolidating social stratifications. In the case I studied, the assessment of students as a part of pedagogical practice constituted an assemblage, where multiple parties, including authorities, education practitioners and migrant workers as students, negotiated and competed for power, and where diverse ideas and practices encountered, diverged, combined and integrated. Only when seeing the assessment as a negotiation process rather than as an indiscriminate practice might we be able to understand its underlying forces and social structures.

Adult academic education such as the Yuanmeng plans seemed to be viewed as inferior to full-time university education both by the general society and the students themselves. This did harm to the learning motivation of the students. In the next chapter, I will further investigate in detail how adult learning affected the aspirations and livelihoods of migrant workers as learners.

8

Adult Learning Practices and Changing Subjectivities

Examining how far the learning practices of migrant workers contributed to their aspirations, livelihood and changing identities presented different responses to the impact of knowledge. A thematic slogan 'Knowledge changes fate while Trade Union helps me shine' was posted in the main conference room of the Home of Migrants College. This college harnessed a range of sources to publicize its achievements in migrant workers' education. Reports and photos about its distinguished alumni were showcased here and there in the building. In addition, Xiao Zhiyuan, my gatekeeper, was kind enough to share with me a collection of alumni's reflective pieces, which would be included in a book on the Haibin Yuanmeng Plan. These narratives were mainly about their learning processes, life stories of vicissitudes and positive changes. However, negative responses to this education plan were also noted in Chapter 5: 'Some people do want to learn something while some others simply want a certificate' (Online interview with Zhao Rong, 05 May 2013).

This prompted me to look at the issue of learning in a more dynamic and open-ended way. The remainder of this chapter analyses multiple implications of 'knowledge' as a discourse in relation to the 'fate' of migrant workers, followed by a discussion of the functions of social connections in the urban experiences of migrant workers and an examination of how the learning of migrant workers was perceived and implemented.

Formulation of subjectivities

Deleuze investigates how subjects come out of discourses and social practices. In illustrating how human subjects evolve, Deleuze, in his collaborative work with Guattari (1983), employs the terms 'desire' and 'desiring machines', and suggests that the subject is nomadic 'with no fixed identity' (17). Deleuze and Guattari (1983) contend that the subject is born as a product of desiring production, and it claims the product and tries to be identified with it. It is in the incessant process of being renovated along with each newly produced state. In other words, there is no definite subject, and what is more, it might be better to say 'subjectivity' instead of 'subject', which is, according to Lorraine (1999): 'the notion of subject as process that must continually repeat itself in order to maintain a specific form and an "economy" or "structuring" of subjectivity to the various means by which a subject can regulate and stabilize this process of being a subject' (ibid, 6).

The subject thus has been in a seemingly stable yet constantly transforming process. I find Foucault's conception on subjectivity in relation to power useful, in the words of Hodgson and Standish: the subject formulation demands 'the identification of the relationship of the subject to power' (2009: 316). This way, subject is derived from power relations and power actions.

The Deleuzian concept of subject and the Foucauldian concept of subject both suggest forces pre-existing individuals. However, I will focus on some dimensions within the forces, including rules, resources, events, social actors and power, in the Social Relations Framework (Kabeer 1994). To explore the relationships between these dimensions, I will use, as a lens, the Deleuzian concept of assemblage, as I did in the previous chapters, to explore how these heterogeneous dimensions and their connections interacted to change the aspirations and the livelihoods of migrant workers as learners.

In addition, Deleuze and Guattari furnish an illuminating explanation on how human subjects psychologically feel when subjectivities change. They believe that when human subjects change, there is 'a schizophrenic experience of intensive quantities in their pure state' that is 'a celibate misery and glory experienced to the fullest' (1983: 18). Bogue (1989) interprets this pure state as an 'pure intensity, an ecstatic torture that makes no differentiation between enjoyment and pain' (72–3). In other words, subjects may experience great pleasure and ecstasy, even in suffering. Deleuze and Guattari (1986) further elaborate on the implications of 'celibate': the celibate machine 'desires solitude', while desiring 'to be connected to all the machines of desire'. Without family or conjugality, the bachelor could become 'all the more social, social-dangerous, social traitor, a collective in himself' (71). Thus, the solitude of the celibate machine contributes to its collectivity and sociality. This celibate misery and glory can be embodied in how my research participants had mixed feelings in their transformations of subjectivities, and how they could be lonely yet hopeful, anticipating their rebirth.

Accordingly, in the case of my research, I will reveal how the subjectivities of migrant workers were formulated and evolved as social products out of education programmes and social practices, involving rules and knowledge, production and distribution of resources, activities, and inclusion and exclusion of social actors.

Knowledge and fate

In exploring how knowledge was related to one's fate, I was guided by Deleuze's concept of assemblage in terms of multiplicity and heterogenous connections. In addition, some of the features from this concept such as fluidity, ephemerality, unpredictability and affective quality (Müller and Schurr 2016: 219) are illuminating.

First, the discourse believing knowledge changes fate appeared to be prevalent. As mentioned above, 'Knowledge changes fate' was a theme in the Home of Migrants College, substantiated by a collection of alumni's reflective writings on this issue. These writings described how alumni were uplifted from the uneducated to the educated, from lower to higher social positions, or from lower to higher aspiration. The following was contributed by Wu Xiaohong from Sichuan Province, southwest China, sponsored by the first year Haibin Yuanmeng Plan in 2008:

> I worked in the daytime while learning in the night time. Life was hard but full. Now I have become an expert in finance management, but I used to be totally ignorant of this field... I am engaged in a trading industry. From my learning experiences, I got to know the similarities and differences between virtual sales and actual sales. A lot of knowledge I learned from my education in the Yuanmeng Plan has been utilised in my work and acknowledged by

my company leaders. It was knowledge that equipped me with wisdom and power and enhanced my self-confidence. I used to be restrained and cautious. But now I am fully enthusiastic with my job, and ready to challenge some work that I had never had courage to think of.

(Wu Xiaohong's reflective piece, collected in 2013)

Wu Xiaohong was named 'representative of image' of the Workers' Quality Enhancement Project of the Haibin General Trade Union, as she was promoted to vice general manager of a logistics company. She attributed her success and aspiration for life to the Yuanmeng education experiences, as she said: 'It was knowledge that equipped me with wisdom and power and enhanced my self-confidence'. This reflective piece appeared to relate knowledge to the changes in her fate.

'Knowledge changes fate', as an institutionalized discourse, was widely accepted. Like Wu Xiaohong, Zhang Li was a distinguished alumnus of the Haibin Yuanmeng Plan. I was able to interview Zhang Li in person, which was different from Wu Xiaohong's case. She was vice general manager of a large property management company, whose headquarters were based in Haibin and which had a lot of branches over a few provinces in China. This enabled Zhang Li to travel around regularly on business. As I said in Chapter 1, I observed a short-term vocational training course on property management. Zhang Li was one of the students in a previous class on this course. Her stories had been told repeatedly by Li Ying, instructor of this course, as an embodiment of 'knowledge changes fate' to inspire his students.

The way I met Zhang Li was dramatic. After a whole day's sessions one day, we happened to find Zhang Li consulting about the Haibin Yuanmeng bachelor's degree courses at the Home of Migrants College. Li Ying warmly invited Zhang Li, me and some other students to have an informal talk in the foyer. This enabled me to understand more of Zhang Li, who came to Haibin from inland Jiangxi Province in 2001 with senior middle school education qualifications, as she recalled:

In the first few years, I did not feel any pressure. Later, when I saw many of my friends and acquaintances having developed themselves, I felt some pressure. So, I read for a property management certificate, and then took a course leading to an associate degree in human resources management.

I felt that if I did not work hard when being young, then there would be no opportunities when getting old.
>
> (Interview notes with Zhang Li, 02 December 2012)

Zhang Li focused on her educational experiences on both academic courses and vocational training courses and attributed her success to her formal learning experiences. Li Ying seemed to align with Zhang Li in his understanding of the positive correlation between knowledge and fate. To illustrate the relationship between knowledge and its impact on Chinese society in one of his sessions, Li Ying put it this way:

> If you do not have academic qualifications, it is hard for you to be promoted. For example, if your boss wants to promote you, but you have only primary school education, then how can they promote you? Would your boss have to bear the stress and pressure from others? They would ask 'Why did you promote her/him rather than someone else?'
>
> (Fieldwork notes, 25 November 2012)

Li Ying used 'primary school education' and outside 'pressure' as examples, so he mainly meant certifications for knowledge. So, though Li Ying did value experienced knowledge, he believed that the knowledge from formal learning was more valued for promotion than that from non-formal or informal learning. Like Li Ying, for Zhang Li and Wu Xiaohong, the knowledge seemed to refer to the knowledge gained from formal learning.

As a form of power, the discourse such as knowledge in relation to fate, in the words of Hodgson and Standish, 'requires and produces particular truths and thereby a particular form of subject' (2009: 316). This suggests that people under the influence of this discourse were reluctant to challenge its authority, let alone overthrow it but identified themselves with it.

Wu Xiaohong had been invited to write a thematic reflection by the Home of Migrants College, so she focused on the contribution of her adult education towards her life. Likewise, Zhang Li, as invited to share some of her experiences with the Yuanmeng Plan, was focused on formal learning. However, over-emphasis on formal learning overshadowed the fact that multiple dimensions and their connections, such as resources and events, other than knowledge alone, were involved in changing migrant workers' trajectory of life and profession. In addition, this tended to neglect other forms of knowledge acquired through informal and non-formal learning.

Secondly, knowledge exists in multiple forms, and is acquired through different channels. It is ambiguous to say 'knowledge changes fate' without differentiating what knowledge was produced by whom for what purposes. Liu Qiang's case is telling. Liu Qiang, a student in the Class of Machinery Engineering, cited in Chapter 7, and a technician of a manufacturing company in Haibin City, was frustrated with the conflict between the demands of his working place and his own learning qualifications:

> I have been working as a technician in Haibin for over fifteen years, but you see I have to study for a certificate. Otherwise, it will be hard to get promoted, as these kinds of opportunities will be given over to those with better academic qualifications. Salaries for the workers in our company are also differentiated according to our academic qualifications. This is just abnormal!
>
> (Interview notes, 14 April 2013)

Liu Qiang's narrative shows that his professional knowledge as an experienced engineer was not fully acknowledged. This sort of knowledge was gained mainly through non-formal and informal learning on the working site rather than in classrooms. Liu Qiang attributed people's over-emphasis on the knowledge acquired through formal learning to abnormal social influence. Consequently, what knowledge would be useful was determined by external discourses and social demands.

Liu Qiang and Li Ying's remarks indicate that different criteria were employed to evaluate differentiated forms of knowledge. There existed a dilemma: while formal learning was more valued by society, the expertise and working skills from non-formal and informal learning were playing a practically vital role in modern enterprises. Liu Qiang's company aligned with the prevalent discourse on the power of knowledge from formal learning. It considered the academic qualifications of its workers and stratified them in terms of wages. This practice was not exceptional Yuanda Province. I discussed how ageism impacted workers and their enterprises in Chapter 3, where a job advertisement also classified workers' wages according to their formal learning background while ignoring other sources of learning or working experiences.

This showed that employers could resort to the discourse around knowledge and fate to strengthen their control over their employees, who could possess good professional skills.

Thirdly, as knowledge is a part of an assemblage, where heterogeneous factors populate, connect and interact, stressing that knowledge changes fate could ignore, either consciously or unconsciously, the workings of other factors and their connections in social processes and the formulation of subjectivities, as is embodied in Zhang Li's case.

Although many other migrant workers took the course of property management, there were not many 'representatives of images' such as Wu Xiaohong and Zhang Li. Zhang Li presented to me a good image of management for a commercial institution. She showed dignity and care in her presentation and communication. She was approachable and friendly yet remained cautious and distanced. To understand her better, I asked her in online chat, 'What about your personality? Do you think it played any role in your promotion?' Zhang Li answered:

> Property management is a service industry. I personally feel that I have natural quality of affinity. This helped me do better in the process of communication with agents and service users. Of course, the point is that we should do our best to be committed to whatever we do. This makes me more confident. In the first year after I joined the Changqing Property Management, I worked hard and won recognition of higher rank authorities, so I was promoted quicker. Now I feel that there are many opportunities for promotion. But knowledge is also important.
> (Online interview with Zhang Li, 10 December 2012)

Zhang Li concluded by emphasizing the vital role of knowledge for her career development, though she admitted the importance of other factors such as her 'natural quality of affinity', 'working hard', 'recognition of higher rank authorities' and 'opportunities', as a line of conditions for her success, including both inherent and external elements. Kabeer (1994) includes in the category of human resources 'the labour power, health and skills of individuals' (280). This shows that knowledge was one of her personal human resources, along with her sociable character and hardworking attitudes, which Zhang Li attempted to separate out as different categories. Some contingent conditions and social connections were also playing a part in Zhang Li's career. The quotes of 'opportunities' and 'recognition of higher rank authorities' indicate that Zhang Li's networking, as an intangible resource, had been well-developed. Zhang Li did not elaborate on what roles intangible resources such as networking played in her promotion, which, however, seemed indispensable for her upward mobility.

Thereby, knowledge needed to be combined with other factors such as her character and attitudes, contingent opportunities and social connections, as knowledge did not work within its own category but connected with heterogeneous factors, considering the principles of 'connection and heterogeneity' (Deleuze and Guattari 1988: 7). Out of the interactions of these factors were produced Zhang Li's aspirations and subjectivities.

Migrant workers such as Wu Xiaohong and Zhang Li, as beneficiaries of adult education, carried forward the belief that knowledge was key to personal development, thus overshadowing the fact that not everybody would be lucky enough to be 'representatives of images', who were a minority of elite people. In analysing knowledge crises in the UK higher education, Barnett (1997) points out there are two categories of knowledge: 'the propositional knowledge produced internally in the academy' and 'knowledge-in-use in the wider world' (ibid, 168). This can be linked to my study: the knowledge that the Yuanmeng students were learning in their classrooms and the knowledge they were using in their workplaces and daily life. So it seemed that the popular discourse 'knowledge changes fate' had been brought into doubt and would need to be rethought and redefined.

Over-emphasizing the power of knowledge without recognizing other relevant factors in contributing to personal and social development could be linked with Street's (1984, 2003) theory on literacy, as cited in Chapter 3. Street (1984) defines two approaches to literacy: the autonomous model and the ideological model. According to Street (2003), the autonomous model suggests that 'literacy in itself – autonomously – will have effects on other social and cognitive practices' and assist learners in 'enhancing their cognitive skills, improving their economic prospects, making them better citizens' (77). However, Street (2003), from the perspective of the ideological model, argues: 'literacy is a social practice, not simply a technical and neutral skill', thus literacy cannot be isolated from 'its "social" effects' (77–8). With these ideas as lenses, I have understood that Zhang Xiaohu, as cited in Chapter 3, seemed to have associated his hardships with his low literacy. He was not able to identify other factors leading to his difficult situations such as limited social connections and inequalities of power, which arose from social and historical practices prioritizing urban areas over rural development. Likewise, understanding literacy as a social practice has lent support to the idea that knowledge was not isolated from other factors including resources, rules and power, but embedded in social practices and relations of power.

Over-reliance on knowledge could be used as an excuse by which some institutions to dodge their responsibility for social justice, which would need an efficient network of social relations rather than relying solely on education and knowledge. Whether knowledge had been fully engaged in empowering migrant workers depended not only on learners themselves but also on other factors such as opportunities and external demands, as Zhang Li's and Wu Xiaohong's narratives show. External conditions and opportunities from society, enterprises and authorities needed to be introduced to transfer the knowledge of migrant workers to practise, as discussed below.

Social connections, underlying rules and adult learning

Guanxi, or social connections in the Chinese context, were active and productive in the life and career of migrant workers. The roles that social connections played in the implementation of the education programmes of migrant workers have been discussed in Chapter 5, where I analysed how social connections and organizations contributed to learning opportunities. Similarly, guanxi, as a social phenomenon in the Chinese culture, remained an interpersonal element among students in their curricular and extracurricular activities. This section aims to examine how far social connections, together with knowledge, were related to the livelihoods and the aspirations of migrant workers.

To inspire his students to study hard, Li Ying quoted a prevalent saying: 'academic qualifications, practical ability, social connections and powerful network are respectively bronze medals, silver medals, gold medals and trump card medals' (Fieldnotes, 25 November 2012). By this, Li Ying attempted to explain what social factors by what underlying rules affected personal promotion. By underlying rules, I mean they were not legally stipulated but socially observed.

The most overwhelming one was a powerful network, seconded by guanxi, or social connections and followed by practical ability. One's knowledge and educational background was the least important of the four factors, as identified by Li Ying. As the powerful network was restricted to a privileged few and inaccessible to ordinary citizens, Li Ying stressed the vital roles of guanxi in social practices and personal development. Although academic learning was cited as the least of the four, it was still an important remedy for the powerless such as migrant workers. Paradoxically, Li Ying cited the saying as a popular opinion, which means that it acted as an ideology itself and could constrain migrant workers' initiative.

Gold, Guthrie and Wank associate guanxi with Bourdieu's concept of social capital, but according to them, this term is more 'negative' than positive, as it could pose a barrier to 'China's becoming a modern society based on the rule of law' (2002: 3). As Liu Qiang complained: 'Wherever you are, you need guanxi. If you are closer to the management, you will get more opportunities' (Interview notes 14 April 2013). Liu Qiang showed his frustration in nurturing guanxi, so he chose to be further educated to change his fate.

Liu Qiang seemed to articulate more of the negative connotations of guanxi. So Liu Qiang and Li Ying brought our attention to the underlying rules, which dictated the complicated and hierarchical society in which education and certificates could be regarded as secondary to one's practical abilities and social relations in certain contexts.

The inter-dependence of different social and personal factors above could be illustrated by the approach of the Social Relations Framework (Kabeer 1994), notably the role of intangible resources such as 'informal networks and association', through which other intangible resources to be produced; in turn, the newly produced intangible resources helped people 'defend or improve their material resource base' (ibid, 280). Then, in the light of this, Zhang Li's status being upgraded could not have been attributed only to her certificates or educational background. As she admitted above, 'I worked hard and won recognition of the higher rank authorities, so I was promoted quicker'. In other words, Zhang Li established strong connections with higher levels of authorities, which laid a good foundation for her upward mobility and enabled her to lead a better life.

Migrant workers were exposed to the influence of a range of dimensions, especially, social connections of different levels. However, when they were not able to gain access to efficient guanxi network, they chose to enhance education qualifications, as Li Ying suggested, thus becoming empowered. However, adult learning, as a part of their life, did not always have clear targets. It is necessary to explore how migrant workers as students treated learning and why, and analyse the social implications existing in the interface between migrant workers and education practitioners, as shown below.

Demystifying the learning attitudes of migrant workers

Discourses on the learning attitudes of migrant workers were diverse and sometimes contradictory. As discussed in Chapter 7, Wang Shaogang, Vice President of the Home of Migrants College, thought that over two thirds of migrant workers as students did not devote enough 'time, energy and money to overcome their difficulties' in their learning process (Wang Shaogang's online college report, 03 December 2012). Likewise, I observed that some students were extremely hard working, though others were seeking to be absent from classes and dodge their duties as students. Thus, I chose not to investigate whether they were lazy but to deconstruct the discourses around 'laziness'. Grillo explains that there is 'a significant distance between the ideas and practices of development agencies and those of "local" people' (1997: 25). This perspective encouraged me to examine the tensions between the discourses and the practices of education practitioners and those of the students and explore the implications embedded within.

Learning 'just in case'

As mentioned in Chapter 3, large-scale companies tended to offer migrant workers as employees more opportunities to be educated. This helped them become more confident and informed, which, in turn, enabled them to have more aspirations.

Meili, again, will be cited here. Having senior middle school qualifications, she entered the Haibin Yuanmeng Plan. After one year's study in a three-year programme leading to an associate degree in economic management initiated at the autumn of 2012, she started to aspire for more knowledge. In addition, her experiences as a coordinator of a bus company enabled her to be sociable and considerate of others. Whether in class time or in a work context, she was welcome and showed a strong spirit of initiative. In my online chat with her in June 2015, I learned that she had obtained her certificate to be a nutrition expert and was taking a course leading her to a status of psychological counsellor, which would cost her 4,500 yuan (450 pounds equivalent). When I asked her why she was learning something totally irrelevant to her job or her degree course, she replied: 'I am planning to learn as much as I can of what I am interested in and within my capacity. You see society is developing. So, I will not fall behind the times. I am learning just in case' (QQ chat record 06 June 2014). Having had enough information in society or organizations was a premise for migrant workers to enter schooling again. In the rapidly developing society, Meili adopted an 'alternative strategy' (Escobar 2007: 21) by opening more choices for her future career.

Similar stories happened in the short-term vocational training courses such as the Property Management Class tutored by Li Ying. More than one student told me they learned it 'just in case' they might need it later, although some of them took it because they were required to produce it to their employers.

Back in the early 1950s, peasants were motivated to learn literacy by having their resentment for the landlord aroused, as noted in Chapter 1. However, migrant workers such as Meili who learned 'just in case' reflected their sense of job insecurity, as 'society is progressing' and 'I will not fall behind the times' indicates Meili's inward anxiety. Students were impacted by the discourses like 'knowledge changes fate'. The learning with the Home of Migrants College enhanced Meili's belief that knowledge could change her life.

However, Meili did not have clear targets to work towards certificates for nutrition and psychological therapy. An online chat with Meili at the beginning of 2020 showed that she continued working with the bus company, working continued undisrupted despite the pandemic of Covid-19 (Online chat with Meili, 16 February 2020).

As mentioned in Chapter 3, I have argued that the Yuanmeng plans were mainly utilitarian education-orientated rather than working towards transformative education in terms of their policy design and implementation. However, in terms of individual learners, I found they had diverging and different purposes. Some students in the Property Management Class took this course as they were required to obtain a certification for job promotion. Concerned about their specific job requirements, they could be utilitarian orientated. However, learning 'just in case' seemed to be directed by transformative learning, as the learners viewed their learning to ameliorate their job prospects.

Not everyone would succumb to the power of knowledge, or to the influence of powerful networks and social connections, as conveyed in Li Ying's quotation above. Consequently, they became 'lazy', as some teachers commented, to be analysed as follows.

'Some students are lazier'

When adult learning was not able to bring about desirable results, migrant workers would take negative attitudes towards their learning. This section will focus on the class of Property Management, as stated above.

As introduced in Chapter 1, the students of this class aimed to work towards a certificate for property management. Li Ying, a man of around fifty years old, treated his students like a father, and was concerned about their coming qualifying examination. He imparted professional knowledge and moral lessons such as treasuring time and studying hard. More than once, he told his students jokingly: 'Spend less time playing cards, smoking, or with lovers, but spend more time in your learning'. As mentioned in Chapter 4, Li Ying was so close to his students that they would not get offended by his remarks or harmless jokes.

In my interview with Li Ying, he said: 'Some students here are lazier than the students in the classes of the same course stationed on other teaching sites, as they do not learn at their own expense. Otherwise, they would have to pay 800 yuan (80 pounds equivalent)' (Interview notes with Li Ying, 25 November 2012). Li Ying suggested that they had not studied hard enough. He had rich experiences in teaching this course on different teaching sites and was thus an influential instructor on property management in Haibin City.

Later, I did observe some 'lazy' students. A student with whom I happened to share a desk had his textbooks clean and unmarked. He admitted shyly that he was too busy to read them, and seldom attended class activities. Students took different attitudes in studying for this course, thus displaying corresponding different degrees of commitment, as not everybody needed the certificate of property management at this moment, though it would be good to have one 'just in case' for the future, as noted above. This was shown in the narratives and experiences from the four students described below.

Liang Dazhi, Zhou Yu, Lu Yang and Yin Meng all came from Henan Province, central China. Liang Dazhi, an estate administrator of a property management company, was the most hard-working student. But Zhou Yu was considering starting or at least being engaged in a company on express delivery, which, he said, was 'much needed in society'. Lu Yang was a lorry driver for a company. Yin Meng, in his early twenties, the youngest of the four, was employed in the same company as Liang Dazhi. He seemed to receive more care from the other three. Here is the description of our first lunch break together:

> Yin Meng showed a lot of respect to me, maybe because I was much older than him while he was the youngest. He said: 'I have no way out. Can you please offer me some suggestions?' This question made me feel guilty as he placed so much trust in me. Liang Dazhi, over thirty years old with experiences of military service, looked much more cautious when talking with me. Hardly had I given a response when he turned us away from this topic. He told me the advantages of taking Yuanmeng course of property management. 'It helps me clarify some issues I did not truly understand. It is a helpful process'. He would tell me this without my questioning him first as he must have thought this was what I wanted from interviewing.
>
> (Fieldnotes, 18 November 2012)

Most of the time, Liang Dazhi was like the spokesman for the Haibin Yuanmeng Plan. On the other hand, Yin Meng felt frustrated by his uncertain future. He spent some years in military service but did not receive enough academic training. In addition, his current job as an administrator in a property management company paid him a monthly income of around 2,500 yuan (around 250 pounds equivalent), which was low in comparison with factory workers. Yin Meng's anxiety was merely a case among the whole generation of migrant workers in Yuanda Province or even other places, but it reflected the general sentiments of quite a percentage of them: to search for a way out for their future, as stated in Chapter 1.

I analysed 'laziness' from different perspectives to show any hidden implications and alternative interpretations. The migrant workers as students like Liang Dazhi were satisfied with their learning opportunities. But some others such as Yin Meng and Zhou Yu were uncertain of their future. They did not seem to count on this course of formal learning for their personal development, but on such alternatives as switching to another job or starting a business of their own. In the words of Deleuze and Guattari, they were ready to face an 'asignifying rupture' (1988: 7–9) from the original assemblage and slide and float onto other assemblages. 'Laziness' was a biased discourse, as this concealed the fact that they were struggling to seek a way out through their education practices.

'You see many students are thinking of quitting'

As mentioned in Chapter 3, the Haibin Yuanmeng Plan, an influential and free education programme for migrant workers, had 'become a well-known brand in Haibin City and even in the circle of All China Trade Union'. I had never thought that quitting the Haibin Yuanmeng Plan could have been an issue. As Robinson-Pant (2000) suggests in her study of Nepali women's literacy education, '"drop out" is a social phenomenon to explore' (161). This inspired me to study why quitting the education programme had happened.

The first time I heard of this news, I was discussing examination content and methods with the students of the Machinery Engineering Class. Liu Qiang, as mentioned above, tried to let me understand the necessity of designing exam papers to an appropriate level. He told me some students were considering giving up this course. I had seen this in their online chatroom but did not take it seriously. As described in the extract from my fieldnotes:

> Liu Qiang said, 'You see many students are thinking of quitting. If you could give me back tuition fees, I will quit'.... I reassured him that their tests they were practising would be useful for the final one, he became quiet. He was

so focused today that he would read aloud in an awkward way, sometimes in a funny loud voice. Some mentioned they paid over 2000 yuan themselves based on the Yuanmeng Plan funding. That is much more than the other Yuanmeng programme.

(Fieldwork notes, 31 March 2013)

The discussion of the students on quitting the programme was mixed up with their anxiety about assessments, deposits and fees. So I took Liu Qiang's remark as a signal of warning that I should make tests easier but the so-called 'many students' was an overstatement. I had not expected quitting to be a noticeable phenomenon. Wang Yan, class mentor, came to the classroom for a class meeting, which was usually given during break time. I sat down and observed:

> Wang Yan said, 'Some students were thinking of quitting. This really surprised me'. Seeing nearly half were absent, she continued, 'If you do not come, how can you pass exams? You are no genius. You should work hard. Remember last semester, nearly half of you failed the maths test. Group leaders should inform students to come. You should play model roles. Just work hard for two more years, and you will get the graduation certificate.... If you do not want to quit, you should concentrate on your study. You should change your personality'.... Wang Yan wanted to appoint some students as group coordinators to replace others, who were absent, but got declined by some nominated ones. She had to readjust her decisions.
>
> (Fieldwork notes, 28 April 2013)

Wang Yan did not concentrate on the problem of quitting the education programme but encouraged her students to study hard when realizing half of the students were absent. This aligned with Li Ying, who believed that some students were becoming 'lazy'. I talked with a man applying for the quitting procedure, staying around the door and waiting for Wang Yan to sign. He said as if shyly and guiltily: 'I am just too busy to continue with this course'. He was doing business in real estate. Usually, he was working at the weekends. This contradicted his formal learning time.

Wang Yan's comments and her students' responses showed that there could be difficulties in asking adult students to play model roles and sacrifice time and energy to collective class activities in today's commercialized society just because they were group leaders, a theme discussed in Chapters 5 and 6. In addition, some students chose to be 'lazy', as half of the students were absent, or even considered quitting their education by excuse of being busy and their jobs and normal life being affected. Therefore, students took 'a line of flight' (Deleuze and Guattari 1988: 9) from the assemblage of formal learning to some other assemblages, as formal learning was not able to change their fate drastically.

This section centralized on the learning attitudes of the students, especially the discourse of students' 'laziness'. However, findings suggest complicated situations were hidden behind this one-sided discourse. Some students learned for this learning itself to prepare for the future but were not certain of its benefits. Others were mainly motivated to acquire certificates. This partly explains why some students became passive in their learning. It seems that formal learning was challenged by social realities. In comparing informal and formal learning, Rogers (2014: 64) states, formal learning 'is felt to be more important because it is visible'. However, some students gave up their formal learning programme to pursue other occupations. This shows that formal adult learning would need to be re-evaluated and combined with other modes of learning, as discussed below, to have its full value realized, recognized and accredited.

Impact of enterprise culture

Every now and then, especially in the early morning when I was in Yuanda Province, I saw service industry workers in uniform and well-formed arrays outside hotels, restaurants or shopping malls, listening to team leaders' instructions. Sometimes, they shouted slogans to cheer themselves up and encourage each other to strengthen their teamwork spirit.

I encountered a report illustrated with a photo on a website (NetEase 2013) in early 2013, describing how a training programme was conducted. Contextualized in Chongqing City, southwest China, and designed to 'develop the endurance of its employees', the trainees, both men and women, were seen crawling in a cyclical line, watched and videotaped by passers-by, subjected to public humiliation. This training put the trainers and the trainees on a specific assemblage, where dominance and obedience were harmoniously integrated into oneness. I could not help relating this scenario to that, as described in Chapter 1, showing the landlords in the Cultural Revolution were chained in a line and persecuted in public.

However, the former group were reconciled to servitude, but the latter despaired and were scared. Foucault, Deleuze and Guattari offer enlightening explanations for such elusive phenomena. In his 'Preface' to *Anti-Oedipus: Capitalism and Schizophrenia*, Foucault (1983) emphasizes that fascism 'causes us to love power, to desire the very thing that dominates and exploits us' (xiii). Deleuze and Guattari (1988) stresses the workings of masochism, asserting that masochism is productive, as the masochist uses 'suffering as a way of constituting a body without organs' (155). Thus, these abnormal behaviours resulted from the interplay of sadism and masochism. This idea is embodied further in the following events, which show subtly the interplay between masochism and sadism disguised in modern enterprise culture.

As mentioned in Chapters 3 and 6, the Class of Economic Management sponsored by the Haibin Yuanmeng Plan prioritized their public image. In their virtual space, photos were posted on students' collective activities. Quite a percentage of the students were attractive and elegant, in good pose and uniforms, like flight attendants, hands held about waists, and delivering a standardized smile. They told me later that they were employees of a bus company. They had received appropriate training in etiquette, including gestures and language use.

I interviewed Lingling, a female student and a bus ticket conductor with the bus company and invited her to share her experiences in on-the-job training. Lingling, as cited in Chapter 3, was always so warm-hearted as to share with me some of her lunch.

> I told Lingling some of my unpleasant experiences in taking a bus and asked her what she would do in a similar case: 'Bus ticket conductors are always pushing, "be quick! Be quick!" What would you do in this case?' Lingling replied, 'We were taught to use proper languages like "Please would you go inside a bit further? Thank you for your cooperation"'.
>
> (Fieldnotes, 31 March 2013)

As stated in Chapter 3, this bus company recommended for the Haibin Yuanmeng Plan course only 'model workers' who had no record of breaking disciplines. Its strict rules and control helped assimilate their employees more. The following observation enabled me to gain deeper understanding of these students on the day of their class outward development, as discussed in Chapter 6:

> The students from the bus company seemed to be very familiar with each other, and they were also most active, sharing food with each other. I was very surprised to find that they had one common feature, that is, their beautiful smile. I knew later that they had received some training on how to smile, like showing 'eight teeth', as one training item in their company.
> (Fieldwork notes, 12 May 2013)

Migrant workers' showing the standardized smile and gesture, as if made from the same mould, suggested that the on-the-job learning enabled them to be assimilated to the rules and culture of their company. Meanwhile, they were optimistic about their public images. In the process of assimilation, a sense of pride, belonging and affectivity was aroused and instilled, as Meili, noted above, often used 'our company' as her catch phrase rather than 'the bus company'. This can be linked with a similar research, contextualized in the organized retail industries in India, exploring how young women from underprivileged class received skill trainings. Findings from this research suggest that despite some negative effects such as surveillance and social censorship, their upskilling trainings and employments elevated their sense of pride and aspirations (Maitra, S. and Maitra, S. 2018).

However, by convincing that some attribute, such as 'showing eight teeth', was a better virtue, the enterprise united while dominating its workers. In turn, the employees lost their unrestrained rural spirit, and became reconciled to the standardized thoughts and behaviours. They gravitated to their enterprise values such as obedience and conformity. Thus, a relationship of hidden slavery, or a body without organs in the Deleuzian sense, was formulated where dominating employers and the dominated employees formulated an assemblage, populated by other heterogenous factors including discourses, resources, people and affectivity.

Declining affectivity in enterprises

The modern sense of slavery unified employees in thought and performances by their enterprise culture. Similar practices existed in the technical training in manufacturing industries: uniformed training for the sake of assembly lines. A comparison shows there have been drastic changes in on-the-job training after the reform and open policy.

As mentioned in Chapter 1, there was an emphasis on national scale adult education and on-the-job training and apprenticeship in the early years after the foundation of P.R. China (Li 1960: 40; Ascher 1976: 19). The practice of apprenticeship was that 'Master workers (*shifu* 师傅) not only imparted to their apprentices' professional knowledge and vocational skills, but also moral lessons on how to conduct themselves. Apprentices were not only assistants of their master workers, but also supposed to look after their master workers' life' (Wang, X. and Zhang, Y. 2015). In other words, master workers and their apprentices were very close in personal relationship, like that of parent and child, and developed personal relationship or *guanxi* (关系). As suggested by Gold, Guthrie and Wank (2002), for this kind of personal relationship, 'there is no time limit for repayments' (7).

At the initial stage of adopting the open policy, as enterprises were mostly state-owned, comprehensive and strict regulations were made to ensure the training of apprenticeships on different levels. In describing how the apprenticeships in China's enterprises were conducted three decades ago, Warner (1986) writes: 'Apprenticeships are normally geared to specialized training. Newcomers are trained for one task, but after several years they can learn other skills. The "production" apprentices are not allowed at first to do repairs, but might do so when qualified' (361). This meant that enterprises were mainly concerned about how to develop apprentices into well-rounded workers with solid skills, thus strengthening the relationship between the management and the staff.

However, my interviews of migrant workers in Lychee City in Yuanda Province from 2012 to 2013 portrayed a different picture of how migrant workers learned their techniques and vocational skills. Most of them were employed by medium- and small-scale privately owned enterprises majoring in labour-intensive manufacturing industry, where large numbers of migrant workers were needed to do mechanically repeated jobs.

Enterprises imposed strict rules and conditions for what kind of workers they needed, such as age limits, educational backgrounds and physical conditions, as stated in Chapter 3. With these points in mind, I interviewed some workers outside in an industrial park where factories were clustered. It was around six evening time. Workers were enjoying their break for around one hour after their supper before resuming their work for a few more hours. I asked a female worker about a job advertisement on a bulletin board. She must have mistaken me for a job hunter, as she looked at me with sympathy, saying: 'Workers are still needed in this factory'. I said, 'But there seem to be limits for workers' ages'. She then gave a grin: 'That doesn't matter. They just say that, but they hire people older than that. I am older than that' (Fieldwork notes, 20 November 2012).

The working conditions and specifications could not be fulfilled by the practical situations on the job market. So the discourse of the conditions represented the images of the workers idealized by the employer.

Factories in Lychee City needed general workers urgently, but often had difficulties in recruiting enough, especially after the Lunar New Year of 2013 when migrant workers returned from their home villages. Various measures were taken to keep them to their original posts. For instance, some factories would not give them the end of year bonus until they were back from this holiday.

My observation of Goods Town, Lychee City was telling. On 24 February 2013, the Chinese Lantern Festival, many stalls emerged suddenly everywhere in the streets to recruit workers, as factories knew workers were coming back from their holidays. In addition, job fairs were frequently held in the town centre, where job agents recruited workers for some companies:

> I noticed a man was very initiative, persuading people to join a company. He looked very cautious when I asked for details. He finally told me he was a recruitment agent for many firms and factories. One young man was discussing with this agent. He wanted to find a job only one month long. The agent answered: 'OK. If you want to leave, let them know three days

before the end of the month. Then you can get wages. Otherwise, there would be some trouble'. Many more were looking at various job ads put up everywhere.

(Fieldnotes, 08 March 2013)

As shown above, the young man simply wanted to do one month. This would mean that his prospective employers would be unwilling to invest a lot in training him. In this case, job training could be short-term, target-specific and simplified. As the woman worker, cited just above, said, 'There are many kinds of jobs. I am just sorting out wires to products. They will tell you how to do. Very easy' (Fieldwork notes, 20 November 2012). Likewise, Wei Jie, eighteen years old, from Guizhou Province, southwest China, offered me similar ideas on how he learned the trade of shoe making with a shoe making plant: 'I learned it on the working site. Watched and learned it. It is not difficult' (Interview notes with Wei Jie, 25 November 2012).

Liansheng, a shop owner of electronic products, provided similar stories. I initially approached him to fix my computer, but we came to understand each other. Liansheng had factory experiences for ten years. Then in 2008, he started to run his own business, dealing in electronic goods, especially computers and accessories. He was the only staff member, acting as boss, manager, technician and shop assistant. When I asked him how he learned computer expertise, he told me: 'I just played it and learned it… Education is useless and expensive' (Fieldwork notes, 26 September 2012). Liansheng could resolve some technical problems. But he seemed to take a trial-and-error method. Quite a few times, I saw him searching online for solutions and downloading some software.

'Watched and learned it' or 'played it and learned it' seemed to be a typical training way for migrant workers with low skills employed by manufacturing enterprises. As Pi's research on migrant workers' education in China (2018) observes, the enterprises, particularly medium- or small-sized ones, do not show willingness to support their migrant employees for all-rounded training, as the trained employees would leave their enterprises or negotiate for a higher income; in addition, training expenditure could be a heavy burden on the enterprises (353). This was different from the complete and well-planned training system among state-owned enterprises in the early 1980s as described above. So it seemed impossible to develop profound social connections between employees and employers or between employees themselves. The so-called traditional guanxi, as displayed with the workers in the early 1950s, was hard to establish and maintain with migrant workers and employers, as there was not much opportunity to invest affective elements into their relationships.

Some critics believe that guanxi brings 'an element of humanity to otherwise cold transactions and comes to the rescue in the absence of consistent regulations or guidelines for social conduct' (Gold, Guthrie and Wank 2002: 3), though this social phenomenon is often associated with its negative side. However, the relationships involving migrant workers in on-the-job training did not appear to contain strong humanity, as these new relationships were connections of 'heterogeneity' and 'multiplicity' (Deleuze and Guattari 1988: 7), interconnecting with any dimension on the same plane constituting heterogeneous factors, including machines, products, commodities, markets, discourses, rules, transactions, virtual spaces and human beings. As employers were concerned about making profits, the impact of the material dimensions, such as machines, products, markets and commodities, overshadowed that of the human factors on the development of guanxi, between employers and employees or between employees. This would be more so in private enterprises employing temporary workers. Inevitably, the affectivity in employer-employee relationship was on the decline. With rapid social and economic development and accelerating commercialization, migrant workers have experienced higher fluidity of job transference across professional fields and geographical areas. This will further reduce the affectivity in modern enterprises and lead to drastic changes in human relationships.

Multiple modes of learning and their accreditation

As noted above, employers and employees did not invest much affectivity into their relationship. One reason was the high fluidity of migrant workers. When I was ready to leave Lychee City in August 2013, I found that, of around twenty security guards of the property management company I met at the start of my fieldwork, only a few stayed, as many new people had joined this company. For instance, Feng Jun, an ambitious security guard, as stated in Chapter 3, had gone back to the German-invested company where he used to work. This section will explore how and what knowledge affected the social and spatial mobility of migrant workers.

My interview described below was conducted in an industrial park in Goods Town, Lychee City around evening time. Amid the moisture of the air, I seemed to detect the smell of sweat. Workers were relaxed: playing badminton, surfing on mobile phones, or simply chatting in twos or threes. I walked up to a group of three people, worried if they would be happy to talk with me. But they were very cooperative after I explained my purpose.

Shu Li, twenty-nine years old, from Shandong Province, eastern China; Wei Jie, eighteen years old, just cited above; and the third young man remaining silent throughout. Shu Li and Wei Jie used to work in the same factory, but Shu Li had transferred to another bigger one for more income. Shu Li was very expressive while concise, with strong communication ability. This was quite different from some other migrant workers I interviewed, but he merely had junior middle school education. I was surprised at his fluency in language ability. He grinned shyly and said:

> It was due to my social experiences outside. I just learned from others. I did not do well when I was a student and had to be outside young… I am not doing so well in comparison with my fellow villagers as they work in Beijing, Shanghai and the Changjiang River Delta. They make more money there.
> (Interview notes with Shu Li, 25 November 2012)

Shu Li's informal learning from his social experiences strengthened his communication skills. He seemed to be the spokesman of the three. Meanwhile, he had wider horizons and was considering reflexively what to improve for his future, as he mentioned his 'fellow villagers' and other places in China. When I asked if there were any education programmes in the factories, Shu Li replied: 'I did not have any training experiences. Just learned on the working site. There are no education courses in factories' (Interview notes with Shu Li, 25 November 2012).

Shu Li's rich experiences in different factories since he came to Lychee City in 2001 were a help with his social and spatial mobility. With junior middle school education and no further formal education, he was able to transfer from one factory to another for more income, after he strengthened his working skills. As Wei Jie agreed, 'You know many people became experienced and then moved to a new place to make more money' (Interview notes with Wei Jie, 25 November 2012).

The upward mobility of migrant workers, such as Shu Li and Liansheng, as mentioned above, was enhanced through their informal and non-formal learning opportunities. Similar evidence has been furnished by research studies in other countries. For instance, Rao and Hossain (2012) conduct research on migrant workers from rural Bangladesh who worked overseas. Their studies show that, in constructing a new identity 'that is socially respected and recognized as successful', these migrant workers benefited from their social experiences which were 'quite distinct from formal schooling, such as their experience of new places and participation in new cultures' (ibid, 426).

Kabeer states that resources and rules are two sides of one coin (1994: 282), as the two dimensions need to be considered simultaneously. Shu Li strengthened his capacity from his working experiences, thus increasing his human resources. Luckily, with relevant social rules, he was able to utilize his resources by transferring freely to another factory, as migrant workers were guaranteed with more power such as minimum wages and labour law, as mentioned in Chapter 3 about Lao Yang's complaint. This, however, means that the power of employers over their employees was reduced.

My analysis so far has been on how informal and non-formal learning, together with relevant social rules, contributed to the development of migrant workers. While migrant workers, such as Shu Li, Wei Jie and Liansheng, acknowledged that social experiences and flexible forms of learning strengthened their social and spatial mobility, Shu Li also admitted his inadequacy of formal learning:

> Of course, it would be better if I had had better educational experiences. A lot of people with poorer educational experiences are not so quick to learn as those with better qualifications. Also, now there are many young people who just graduated from vocational schools and then joined the working force. They are undoubtedly challenging to the workers with lower education qualifications.
> (Interview notes with Shu Li, 25 November 2012)

Shu Li perceived the challenges coming from younger people with formal vocational qualifications, as he was 'not so quick to learn'. This suggests that the formal learning experiences, with systematic and intensive training, provided learners with solid foundation and lasting influence.

Like Shu Li, Yin Fa also offered similar narratives. Yin Fa, in his late thirties, from Shaanxi Province, northwest China, ran a stall selling grilled food in Goods Town, Lychee City, and his business was welcome to many young customers. Unlike some stall owners offering food by hand, he used tongs and brown bags to deliver food. This greatly enhanced the image of his food business. As my interview proceeded on his working site, I would be an assistant when he was busy. After a few interviews, we came to understand each other more. Once he told me: 'I respect people like you, as you are better educated, but I have only had junior middle school education. This posed a barrier to my understanding and further promotion in factories' (Interview notes with Yin Fa, 9 December 2012).

In 2007, Yin Fa came to Lychee City and found employment with a factory making computer accessories. Usually, he worked in the daytime and used one hour in the evening time learning relevant theories and practical operation. To remedy for his lack of working skills, he did not care about the dirt or hard work. This way, he won trust from his boss. He sometimes would be assigned to over ten machines, which would bring several hundred yuan more monthly income than others. However, as mentioned above, he was not well educated. So, when he was likely to be promoted to the post of director in the office, he lost the chance, as there were well-educated younger people flooding into the job market, who had earned formal vocational certificates. So he decided to leave this plant after working there for three years and transferred to another factory. However, as described by Yin Fa: 'Work remained as tiring as ever. I did not like that feeling with machines humming, rumbling and banging around. Even today, I seem to be hearing the noises around me. I resigned again one year later in 2011 and began to do my own small business like this' (Interview with Yin Fa, 14 December 2012).

Yin Fa was very disappointed yet relieved. Remaining loyal and devoted to his enterprise, he had not been able to gain a promotion, which was, instead, given over to younger people with qualifications gained through formal learning. Inadequate formal learning put him at a disadvantage in comparison with the newly joined employees. He decided to leave the manufacturing industry, which did not prioritize older workers, as also stated by Feng Jun in Chapter 3.

This substantiates the idea that, in comparison with informal and non-formal learning, formal learning was still dominating in the mainstream ideology. As Rogers (2014) observes, formal learning is related to a formal education or training institution with clear learning objectives (15), which makes it sound 'more important because it is visible' (64). This point is also strengthened by the job advertisement, as analysed in Chapter 3, which promised different levels of income to workers according to their education qualifications, as well as by Liu Qiang's narratives earlier in this chapter.

Then there seemed to exist a paradox: on the one hand, employers wanted to hire better educated staff while utilizing the human resources of the lower educated ones such as Yin Fa and Shu Li. In this sense, the qualifications gained through formal learning were deployed as a discourse by the employers to control their employees ideologically.

Yin Fa, unlike Liansheng, noted above, did not claim 'education is useless'. However, he made up his mind to escape from his past and become a new self. Factory experiences, a painful memory, enriched his knowledge around urban society through non-formal and informal learning. This enabled him to realize that he had been working for others. He needed to be independent, as Liansheng had already done. He was running a small stall. But he was more aspiring than this, as his next plan, when next spring returned, was to run a restaurant in Lychee City or back in his home county.

Formal, non-formal and informal learning each plays an important role in adult knowledge learning; however, they are inseparable from each other. As Rogers (2014) argues, 'informal and formal learning may be seen as lying on a continuum' (21). The education programmes in the Yuanmeng plans were formal learning programmes that would lead migrant workers as learners to university certification and accreditation. On the other hand, informal learning and non-formal learning were an indispensable part of the learning, as 'Measures of adult competencies... support the idea that learning takes place over the life course and not only during childhood or within schools' (UNESCO 2015: 131).

So, for migrant workers, such as Wei Jie and Shu Li, non-formal learning on-the-job site, as an intentional practice, offered them opportunities to learn transferrable job skills so that they were able to transfer to different working places. Likewise, the informal learning of migrant workers, such as Liansheng, who 'played it and learned it', and Fang Xu, as cited in Chapter 3, who worked as an active volunteer for a drama club speaking for migrant workers in Haibin City, was immersed in urban daily life, experiences and routine work.

Somewhat different, Chuan Aixiang exemplified how one was able to blend multiple modes of learning. As described in Chapters 3 and 5, Chuan Aixiang was awarded a bachelor's degree in Mechanical Engineering by Hubei Innovative University in Hubei Province in 2013. Meanwhile, he accumulated rich working experiences with a few foreign-invested companies in Haibin City. At the beginning of 2019, he transferred to Lychee City from Haibin City and was employed as a senior engineer with a large company. Chuan Aixiang's life history suggested that multiple modes of learning constituted a dynamic and inseparable process. This finding could be used to exemplify UNESCO's anticipation of lifelong learning in the future that 'Formal, non-formal and informal learning activities pervade all spheres of life, including work, family, civic engagement and leisure' (UNESCO 2020: 12). However, it would not be enough to acknowledge the impact of migrant workers' blended learnings for individual and social development. Their learning experiences and value need to be further recognized by society, enterprises and institutions, locally, nationally and even globally. This understanding has found support from the goal envisioned by UNESCO (ibid, 12) for the lifelong learning by 2050: 'legal foundations and mechanisms have been established for the recognition, validation and accreditation of learning outcomes acquired in different contexts'. The realization of this goal would bring great conveniences to migrants for their personal living and contribute to socioeconomic development in an international context.

This section shows that informal and non-formal learning gained from social practices contributed to the social and spatial mobility of migrant workers. The mobility process was facilitated by changed governmental labour laws and a favourable social atmosphere. Meanwhile, findings suggested that higher formal learning could promote the further development of migrant workers, though it is worthwhile to note that lack of formal learning could serve as an ideological control on migrant workers.

Ever-changing and nomadic subjectivities

This chapter studied how adult learning and urban experiences impacted the livelihoods and aspirations of migrant workers and how their subjectivities were shaped out of the interactions amid heterogenous dimensions such as rules, resources, events and social actors. Findings suggest that there existed a social tendency to over-emphasize the knowledge acquired through formal learning. This overshadowed the importance of other dimensions such as informal and non-formal learning and social connections in job transference and social mobility of migrant workers.

Migrant workers had learned to be social persons and better for survival in urban areas through their social experiences. However, biased support for formal learning could harm the aspirations of migrant workers of lower education qualifications but strong practical capacity, such as Shu Li and Yin Fa, thus deteriorating social inequity and increasing a sense of job insecurity. This was revealed where Meili spoke of the purpose of her taking a psychology course as 'just in case'. This could be linked to the idea of Bourdieu and Passeron (1990), who asserted that 'credentials contribute to ensuring the reproduction of social inequality by safeguarding the preservation of the structure of the distribution of powers through a constant redistribution of people and titles characterized' (xi).

In a rapidly changing society in China, formal learning for adults should be regarded as only one of the constituents contributing to social, personal and economic development. The subjectivities of migrant workers as learners as well as their aspirations and achievements were formulated out of diverse dimensions and their interactions. Through constant negotiation in discourses and social practices, they were becoming new selves.

So it seems understandable that Liansheng claimed 'education is useless and expensive', as he had his own choices. Migrant workers had to make constant decisions as to when to break with the present assemblage and where to go for the next one. In this process, they assumed flowing identities: workers, peasants and small business owners, in the case of Yin Fa, or workers, peasants and security guards, in the case of Feng Jun. But they had 'no fixed identity', to use the words of Deleuze and Guattari (1988: 17). Thus, assemblages of heterogenous factors such as resources and rules provided processes, out of which new subjectivities were constructed.

To conclude this chapter, let me invite Yin Fa back. With the approach of the Lunar New Year festival of 2013, Yin Fa decided to go back to Shaanxi Province, where he had been away for four years. He was missing his parents and a child left behind to his parents. He might come back to Lychee or simply stay in his home county. He told me: 'The development of west China is ongoing. So, Shaanxi Province, where Xi Jinping's ancestors came from, will be better developed soon'. Tears welled up in his eyes. Pain and ecstasy merged within him, as a new self was being formulated. This mental state was perceivable, as it was, in the words of Deleuze and Guattari, 'a celibate misery and glory experienced to the fullest' (1988: 18). So personal dreams of ordinary citizens such as Yin Fa and the national Chinese Dream, elaborated by Xi Jinping, the president of China, as discussed in Chapter 3, re-echoed each other.

In exploring the relationship between education and its outcome, I did not focus on the linear cause and effect relationship between them but tried to explore their multiple and dynamic connections. This was different from the economist approach adopted in research studies conducted by researchers such as Psacharopoulos and Patrinos (2004) and Montenegro and Patrinos (2013). Psacharopoulos and Patrinos (2004), 'based on the fix provided by the newer quasi-experimental research on the economics of education', argued that 'investment in education behaves in a more or less similar manner as investment in physical capital' (118). Accordingly, Montenegro and Patrinos (2013) concluded in their report for the World Bank that 'the returns to schooling continue to be healthy, at about 10 per cent a year globally' (10). Thus, the causal relationship between returns and investment in schooling was reduced to a percentage.

However, in investigating the relationship between education and migrant workers, I was concerned how a multiplicity of dimensions such as rules, resources, events, power and people interconnected and interacted in these education processes. Thus, I explored how multiple forms and implications of knowledge interacted with other factors such as social connections and social rules, which contributed to the transformation of the subjectivities of migrant workers.

9

Assemblage, Tensions and Social Change

My fieldwork experiences in Yuanda Province presented assemblages, where were populated heterogeneous factors such as people, events and discourses. I had thought about bringing together all the research participants to this conclusion. This turned out to be impossible. We used to be on the same assemblage, but most of us slid and entered onto different assemblages, experiencing new trajectories of life. People could choose to break with the assemblage, as our affectivity declined over space and time.

However, I was able to map out life trajectories of some major participants. Older and married migrant workers with children, such as Liang Dazhi, Meili and Zhao Rong, were determined to be settled in Haibin City. But younger unmarried ones could be more fluid. For instance, Wen Xiangyang, as cited in Chapters 2 and 5, left Haibin City in 2017 for Suzhou City, east China and worked as a salesman with a company producing electrical appliances. At the beginning of 2021, he told me that he had returned to his hometown in Anhui Province, to 'find employment with a local enterprise while supporting and gaining support from family members'. In fact, as stated in Chapter 1, increase in migration to major large cities seemed to have stopped from 2014 onwards (Gregory and Meng 2018: 396). As more local enterprises have been established and income gap between coastal areas and inland areas has further narrowed down, more and more migrant workers have started to seek employment near their home counties rather than migrate across provinces.

Increasingly developed digital technologies have connected me with the Yuanmeng plans. I have witnessed how the Yuanmeng plans have been developing for the past ten years. A report on the Haibin Yuanmeng Plan for the year of 2020 brought me back to the familiar discourses against the background of the Covid-19 pandemic:

> For the past 13 years, the Yuanmeng Plan has been constantly developing. There has been an accumulated investment of 110 million yuan in this programme ... The Yuanmeng Plan is a sincere gift from Haibin City to the hard-working people. It shows full respect from the city for knowledge, dreams and fighters ... The Yuanmeng Plan for this year is especially of significance in times of containing the Covid-19 pandemic and returning to normal production and work. It has endeavoured to provide learning opportunities for those who genuinely need them, thus it tends to offer support to those enterprises and workers which have been severely impacted by the pandemic... to make contribution to the overall socioeconomic development ...
>
> (the Haibin General Trade Union 2020)

The Haibin Yuanmeng Plan continued its original principle of assisting the needy workers and was carrying on its initial spirit and dreams while going forward with the times. Meanwhile, the Yuanda Yuanmeng Plan has also been developing steadily, as stated in Chapter 1, with participating educational institutions increasing to forty-three in total, providing learning service and support in a range of cities and towns over the whole province. These two education initiatives have won publicity and recognition on social media nationwide. The chapter brings together the issues discussed previously, recaps major research findings and puts forward some policy implications.

The concept of assemblage as a perspective

One of the moves that spurred me to write about migrant workers, as stated at the beginning of Chapter 1, was a string of suicides of young migrant workers in a Foxconn factory in 2010. In addition, I had noticed there was a tendency to relate education with social progress, migrant workers' aspirations and social practices. 'Knowledge changes fate' had been a prevalent discourse for decades. However, complex realities made me understand that this issue was not a linear cause and effect but involved multiple dimensions. To present the complex ideas involving multiple relationships and heterogeneous factors was a difficult project. The reading of the Deleuzian concept of assemblage, the approach of Kabeer's Social Relations Framework (1994) and the approach of development as discourse furnished me with useful tools to explain and express my thoughts, which would be otherwise chaotic.

The concept of assemblage as well as its relevant ideas has run throughout this book. Although I was aware that an assemblage involves many factors, I was mainly using the five dimensions of resources, rules, people, events and power in the approach of the Social Relations Framework (Kabeer 1994) to make my analysis operable and focused. However, I included other factors as well to stress fluidity, multiplicity and ephemerality derived from the concept of assemblage. I was also inspired to interpret some findings in terms of affectivity, for example the declining affectivity in workers' relationship and changes of subjectivities as discussed in Chapter 8.

The concept of assemblage prompted me to rethink and reinterpret why the second-generation migrant workers were considered to be 'fragile' (All Trade Union Report 2010), as stated in Chapter 1. After the reform and opening in China in the 1980s, the first-generation migrant workers slid and floated between different assemblages. They were able to go back to their home villages, where their children, parents and wives were left behind. On the other hand, they could choose to migrate to the city, where they were working to make money and then send it home. Consequently, they would always have a place where to rest their minds. However, the second generation concentrated on the urban assemblage. Many of them dreamed to be settled in the city, thus losing the way back to their home villages. This, in a sense, restricted their choices for where to live and they became more subject to frustration and despair.

The concept of assemblage also made me reflect why a string of suicides were attempted with Foxconn Technology Group, as noted in Chapter 1. As migrant workers were on an assemblage which could be described as associations of human and non-human elements (Müller and Schurr 2016: 217), they were impacted by these dimensions and their connections, especially the dehumanizing machines they worked with as assembly line workers. To explain how these machines impacted the well-being of migrant workers, I find illuminating the concept of becoming by Deleuze and Guattari (1988) which is defined as that which 'constitutes a zone of proximity and indiscernibility'

(293–4). The relationship incorporating workers and assembly lines could be interpreted as a zone of proximity and indiscernibility between machines and human beings. 'Machines humming, rumbling and banging around', as narrated by Yin Fa in Chapter 8, were on the same assemblage with workers, impacting their physical and mental state. Assembly lines and workers, along with sounds and products, worked away into a preverbal state of chaos, where non-human factors were dominating.

In a similar vein, as stated in Chapter 1, Xu Lizhi, a poet and a migrant worker with Foxconn Group, presented us with the harrowing poem, 'My lost time, toilsome as assembly lines', which formulates an assemblage where events of 'sold' and 'packed' connected 'time', 'assembly lines' and 'ocean'. However, the poet, as a human being, seemed to have vanished and the human affectivity on this plane was diminishing, as there appeared to be hardly any human or living elements on this assemblage. Thus, the poet had formulated a zone of proximity and indiscernibility with dehumanizing factors where non-human elements dominated. Sadly, he was not able to gain enough force to escape from this assemblage to enter a new assemblage.

However, the moment when the death of Xu Lizhi happened there existed chances of the rebirth of his subjectivity, through which he could have risen above his old self and transformed into a new subject. This was the moment of 'a celibate misery and glory experienced to the fullest', to use the words of Deleuze and Guattari (1983: 18), as discussed in Chapter 8. Deleuze and Guattari further analyse the workings of this critical moment: 'Subjectification carries desire to such a point of excess and unloosening that it must either annihilate itself in a black hole or change planes'. (1988: 34). In the light of this idea, we could say that Xu Lizhi had been faced with two choices: either total breakdown or a flight onto a new plane to become a new self. Thereby, if people such as Xu Lizhi had gained any intervention of any measure or new connections with new discourses, social connections, job opportunities and affection, they could have risen into a brand-new self in the way caterpillars tear open the cocoons encaging them and become butterflies.

The concept of assemblage explains how I was able to conduct a multi-sited fieldwork and analyse the data emerging from within it. I slid and floated across assemblages constituted by different people, rules and resources. I felt the strong affect on and across the assemblages, which pushed me to do this research and complete it. Thereby, I have been transforming out of these experiences and interactions into new subjectivities.

Adult learning and social change

In investigating how education programmes were related to adult development and aspirations, I did not find a linear cause-effect relationship but uncover complex relationships and findings. Likewise, the dialogue between my prior knowledge and theoretical learnings, as introduced in Chapter 2, changed how I interpreted my research data. I will recapitulate my major findings as follows.

Firstly, the Yuanmeng education programmes for migrant workers had empowered some migrant workers and enhanced their aspirations. They contributed to local education and socioeconomic development by socializing and commercializing educational resources. However, they also led to stratifying migrant workers. Such large-scale degree programmes for adult learners were only administered in Yuanda, an economically developed area. There do not seem to have been similar projects for adult workers elsewhere. This could further increase the regional disparities in economic and social development. In addition, as concluded in Chapter 8, migrant workers as students in Yuanda Province were influenced by diverse dimensions such as social connections and informal, non-formal and formal learning. Biased emphasis on formal learning such as the Yuanmeng plans affected the aspirations of some migrant workers with lower academic qualifications yet strong professional competency. This trend could cause unfair redistribution of resources and opportunities for social mobility, thus creating further social stratification within migrant workers. This finding can be linked to a research conclusion that 'education continues to play a crucial role in social stratification in contemporary China' (Du 2016: 173). Du's research is on the general education in China while my study is on adult education. Similar to Du's idea, my study on migrant workers' education suggests that adult education in China, such as the Yuanmeng plans, could contribute to stratifying migrant workers and increase the inequalities among themselves.

Secondly, as top-down programmes, the education practice of the Yuanmeng plans could be related to the literacy campaign in the 1950s, as it was able to mobilize efficiently human and financial resources to provide study places for many learners. This practice was further strengthened with the aid of digital technology. However, the education design was more based on policy designers' understandings and intentions of what these programmes should be like and how they should be implemented, as they did not seem to present strongly marked features typical of the education for migrant workers. Except for some short-term vocational and functional courses, the Yuanmeng plans were mainly featured with their academic programmes. Their teaching contents appeared to have transplanted full-time courses provided by degree-awarding universities and implemented over a large number of migrant workers as learners by modern distance-learning technology. This practice neglected the individual needs of migrant workers as learners but saw them as abstract numbers engaged in an education process, as the Yuanmeng plans mainly served to urbanize migrant workers for the utilitarian purpose of urban social development rather than for their personal development.

What is more, the Yuanmeng plans, as public events, have brought about social impact by being actively engaged in social practices and discourses. However, education qualifications have served as a way of exerting ideological control over migrant workers. Some migrant workers, such as Liansheng (Chapter 8), dismissed adult education as 'useless'. There were, however, more migrant workers, such as Zhang Li, who stressed the vital role of knowledge in her career development (Chapter 8), and Zhang Xiaohu, who ascribed his poor working conditions mainly to his low academic qualifications (Chapter 3). They related the changes in their life and career to their educational experiences. This understanding suggests that academic qualifications could be 'legitimating the reproduction of the social hierarchies' (Bourdieu and Passeron 1990: 152–3) among migrant workers. In such a context where discourse such as 'the power of knowledge' was prevailing, academic qualifications not only could mean knowledge but could also be utilized by any sector or enterprise as a dominating ideology or a management discourse.

Tensions and contradictions from policy to practice

In exploring the Yuanmeng plans from their policy to practice, I analysed the tensions and contradictions existing in discourses and events. For instance, the concept of development as discourse explores the relationships and discrepancies between local knowledge and development interventions (Grillo 1997; Escobar 2007). Tensions could be found in Foucault's understanding of power as inertia and dynamism (Gordon 2020). Likewise, Deleuze and Guattari investigate how desire is shown in both sadism and masochism (1988: 155), as applied in Chapter 8.

It remained my central concern to examine tensions and contradictions from a microlevel to a macrolevel. These were shown in a range of links and aspects, such as the naming of Yuanmeng plans, student recruitment rules, curriculum design, pedagogical practice, teacher selection, student assessment and enterprise culture. Ideologies in adult learning in Yuanda Province seemed to be a central concern for policy makers and education providers. In addition, the workings of ideologies were also observed in education practice. However, the ideologies did not always bring about desired consequences. Thus, there existed some tensions and contradictions between these discourses and their practices.

Firstly, tensions and contradictions existed between administrative and ideological control and commercialized practices. As stated in Chapter 1, the education on thought and politics played a vital role from 1950s to 1970s in China's education. This remained so in the policy of Yuanmeng plans. As shown in Chapters 3 and 4, the leadership of the Communist Party of China was stressed in policy design and education practice. For instance, the aim of the Yuanda Yuanmeng Plan was to transform learners into a working force that the Communist Party of China could rely on. To achieve this, Lychee Municipal Communist Youth League Committee planned to nominate its cadres to join and strengthen the teaching force of Lychee Waterfront University. In a similar vein, the Haibin Yuanmeng prioritized thought and politics in their total curriculum, which included a range of courses for migrant workers (Chapter 3).

However, the two programmes were marked with distinctive features of commercialism, as discussed in Chapters 3–7. For instance, commercial discourses were used in promoting programmes, commercialized devices for student recruitment, and commercialized management in curricular and extracurricular activities. The commercialization trend noted in my research studies can be linked with similar developments in higher education internationally over the past decades. As Barnett (1997) notes, higher education in the UK 'has been subject to the marketization of the welfare state', as 'students become customers for courses now marked as products' (ibid, 168). As for vocational education, the trend of commercialization seems not to be a current trend but to have been lasting for a number of decades. Similarly, Lowe (1999), as cited in Chapter 7 on assessment of students, argues that the producers of some international curricula and qualifications have made contribution 'in the commodification of education, in its incorporation into global capitalism' (329). Lebeau and Bennion (2014) also point out the economic difficulties of universities in the most peripheral regions of the UK, which need to 'compete for students on both local and global markets' (290). Therefore, education, together with other economic and cultural sectors, has joined the commercialization process on a global scale. As stated earlier in this chapter, the Yuanmeng plans have been developing steadily for the past ten years. This has brought together more educational institutions as partners and exhibited strong features of commercialism. Thus, the Yuanmeng plans have become a part of an international market of education.

In addition, tensions and contradictions arose between curriculum and its practice with the Home of Migrants College. The curriculum required that the interactive teaching be adopted, as admitted by the teaching staff and relevant documents. However, the actual teaching remained teacher centred. The interactions between teachers and students were more symbolically conducted than persistently implemented. One of the reasons that hindered this approach from being fully employed could be the large class sizes. Equally interesting, while collectivism was advocated in the curriculum, individualism was practised in its implementation. As discussed in Chapter 4, teachers in the Haibin Yuanmeng Plan were encouraged to observe collectivism and make sacrifices for the well-being of the college. Likewise, extracurricular activities, as analysed in Chapter 6, were employed to develop students' awareness of collectivism and cooperation. However, these ideas, which used to be well embraced from 1950s to 1970s, were not fully accepted by every individual, as some staff chose to enter a different area for personal development while some students did not demonstrate strong desire for collective activities. The tensions between individualism and collectivism, or between commercialism and socialism, are increasing in the age of globalization and digitalization. As stated in Chapter 1, Xi Jinping, the president of China, emphasizes the 'normalization and institutionalization of the education of ideals' and argues for the importance of the education of patriotism, collectivism and socialism (2020). Thus, how to build social confidence and cohesion by advocating and practising collectivism and socialist ethos remains an issue for the state and the government.

Thirdly, tensions and contradictions existed between the discourses on knowledge and other dimensions for one's aspirations and success. As noted in Chapter 8, discourses on knowledge and learning, acquired through formal learning, impacted migrant workers as learners so that some of them prioritized the role of knowledge for their upward mobility. This propelled migrant workers as learners such as Meili and Zhang Li (Chapter 8) to be identified with the idea that 'knowledge changes fate'. Thus, Meili was learning for more certificates bearing no relation to her job 'just in case' while Zhang Li, an 'image representative' of the Haibin Yuanmeng Plan, considered knowledge as the foremost dimension for success.

However, the knowledge acquired through formal learning has been challenged by the knowledge and skills acquired through the informal and non-formal learning from on-the-job experiences, as well as migration experiences as a learning process. For instance, some migrant workers as learners, such as Liu Qiang, as shown in Chapter 8, had to take formal education for a certificate, although they were competent in their professions. So, they questioned the necessity of taking academic courses. This suggested that the knowledge learned through formal learning had become only one of the multiple forms of knowledge along with other forms of practical skills and knowledge. Likewise, a close reading of Zhang Li's life history shows she did not state some other vital dimensions for her promotion until questioned, such as strong social connections, non-formal and informal learning and contingent opportunities. This shows, while knowledge made positive contributions to upward mobility, its related discourses formulated an ideology that could become a barrier to understanding its limitations.

The interrelationships between formal, non-formal and informal learning, as examined in Chapter 8, as well as tensions and contradictions around online learning and face-to-face learning in Chapter 5, could be linked with the UNESCO's (2020) goal for lifelong learning by the year of 2050: integrate recognition, validation and accreditation mechanisms and establish a 'collectively built global learning ecosystem', including formal, non-formal and informal learning, as well as diverse learning modalities (8–12). The establishment of these mechanisms will be able to bring together different societies and communities all over the globe and provide conveniences for migrants to fully use their skills and knowledge.

Policy makers, education practitioners and researchers

I have researched policy making, education practice and outcomes of education of the Yuanmeng plans that were focused on migrant workers in Yuanda Province. I have provided an analysis of the multiple relationships involving educational stakeholders and the transforming ideologies and social practices within and across the education of migrant workers. In this section, I will attempt to draw out policy implications.

Firstly, the Yuanmeng plans, as large-scale government-sponsored education programmes, have become more and more influential year by year. But there seems to be a lack of academic research conducted on the implementation of these intervention programmes. As mentioned in Chapter 2, I did meet, by chance, a researcher who gave out questionnaires to students I was teaching, and then left soon after collecting them. So education practitioners appeared to be, as shown in the case of the Home of Migrants College, interested in writing reports and presenting students' positive testimonials to win publicity. Likewise, policy makers and officials seemed to feel suspicious of the outside researcher, as revealed in Chapter 1 describing how I searched for fieldwork sites for the Yuanda Yuanmeng Plan. This book has demonstrated the necessity and the potential for policy makers, education providers and researchers to work more closely in assessing policy making, education practice and research to further improve their teaching and research.

Secondly, the book illustrates how authorities within and across the educational field of migrant workers took a leading role in funding collection and allocation, policy making and design, and deciding educational partnerships. The findings point to the need to consider implementing education projects by coordinating stakeholders. However, excessive intervention such as random designation of partnership educational institutions could damage educational processes, as shown in Chapter 3. In this process, local government, as education policy makers and donors, could be faced with a dilemma: either encouraging the development of local educational institutions or giving the development opportunity over to more competitive outside institutions. It must make feasible plans to balance the development of the local institutions and the impact of the outside institutions. What is more, the government may need to consider how to make education plans that will be truly fair and inclusive of every eligible citizen, regardless of their age and household register, and which are able to satisfy learners' both practical and symbolic needs.

In addition, my analysis has shown how both education providers such as the Home of Migrants College and migrant workers as students thought they were not receiving 'real' university education and felt diffident about what job opportunities their education would bring to them. This showed their identity crisis as university students. As the Yuanmeng plans were mainly focused on academic programmes, which were essentially a simplified version of the full-time education curriculum, education providers would need to consider how to establish their own features in terms of teaching force, teaching content and pedagogical practice, and how to win recognition from the public. As shown in the analysis of pedagogical practice in the Home of Migrants College, different discourses and perceptions existed around curriculum practice. This suggests that education practitioners would need to consider how to manage educational processes that are being developed, such as adapting traditional teaching ideas to the commercialized society, reconciling online learning with face-to-face learning, diversifying assessment methods rather than employing grades and scores only, and encouraging creativity by combining collectivism and individualism. Some of these ideas have already been in practice. For instance, online learning and face-to-face learning have been rapidly integrated, and their relationship has been further consolidated with the outbreak of the Covid-19 pandemic. For another instance, the exploration to design appropriately practicable assessments has always been an issue, particularly in times of digitalization. Thus, it seems to be a constant dilemma to reconcile similar tensions and contradictions embedded within assessment processes, as detailed procedures involved in reconciling these tensions and contradictions still need to be investigated.

What is interesting, I have noted the difficulties that commercial educational institutions face as well as agencies engaged in adult education such as Lychee Seabreeze Academy (see Chapter 3). Although they were not the focus of my research, they played a vital role in the commercial society by connecting students with educational institutions by making important investment in education. But they still need government support and development opportunities.

Finally, as shown in my empirical chapters, especially in Chapter 8, the informal and nonformal learning helped migrant workers and enterprises in many ways, such as learning transferrable skills and guaranteeing substantial working force. However, their importance was not fully recognized by society, enterprises, or even migrant workers themselves. Traditional apprenticeship, as mentioned in Chapter 8, which involved strong personal relationships and feelings between experienced and new workers, seemed to be disappearing, notably in the private medium and small enterprises. This can be even more so now. These enterprises did not have strong motivation to make well-rounded workers of their employees but merely to enable them to complete certain parts of work required on the production line. Therefore, it is necessary to consider how to resolve the discrepancies in terms of development aims between employers and employees, especially migrant workers as employees.

When recommending training systems as those used in Germany, King (1993) suggests that a good training system should involve 'a complex negotiation about the roles of the state, the employers and the unions' (214). Some research studies (e.g. Pi 2018; Wang and Chen 2021) argue for the shared governance engaging the government, enterprises, migrant workers and education providers in migrant workers' learning in China. On this basis, I would further suggest that all parties on the assemblage of migrant education in China, government, employers, education providers, researchers and migrant workers, would need to work together and make contributions to social development as well as to the personal development of migrant workers.

The book as a factor of assemblages

My research was inspired by my wish to share my understanding of migrant workers in China. This impulse was consolidated by my personal feelings for migrant workers in my ancestors' home county in central China, thus prompting me to consider migration in a general sense. Then I moved on to continuing education for migrant workers in Yuanda Province in south China to study how far adult learning was related to the development and aspirations of migrant workers.

Consequently, I have attempted to explore the relationship between education for migrant workers and their aspirations and ideas of education development. I found that there was no linear cause and effect relationship between these two polarizations. In the research process, I have tried to go beyond quantitative statistical analysis by drawing on rich ethnographic data to explain the implementation processes of education programmes and the learning processes of migrant workers.

To be freed from the deceptive power of discourses and knowledges, Kabeer suggests the idea of 'conscientization' (1994: 299), elaborated by Freire in his *Pedagogy of the Oppressed* (1970). However, in the context of my research, I would not say it would be enough to resort to critical awareness to bring about desired educational and social changes amid educational stakeholders. The changes mainly result from assemblages, where external connections of heterogeneous factors are made and where resides the fundamental driving force for changes.

The whole process from policy to practice in terms of the education programmes and the learning of migrant workers involved assemblages of heterogenous factors such as rules, resources, people, events, power and affectivity. These factors were mutually connected, producing tensions and contradictions. These tensions and contradictions, along with other factors, interacted, negotiated, ruptured or coalesced, which propelled the implementation of the education programmes and contributed to the changes of policy makers, practitioners and migrant workers as learners in their ideology, their educational practice and their ever-changing subjectivities.

Once I began to write this book, I have made connections with its virtual readers through this writing practice. As Deleuze and Guttari write, 'the book is not an image of the world. It forms a rhizome with the world, there is an aparallel evolution of the book and the world' (1988: 11). Likewise, this book has become a link of the assemblages, which have involved myriad factors: ideas, resources, events, and you, the reader, and which will encourage further dialogue and thought on learning and social change.

Notes

Chapter 1

1. All the Chinese-English translations in this book are conducted by the author of this book unless otherwise stated. The original Chinese version of this poem is as follows:

   我像流水线一样辛苦的光阴,
   和最新款手机一起打包
   贩卖到大洋彼岸,
   等候下一个轮回。

2. All the names concerning people, places and institutions related to my fieldwork are pseudonyms to protect the privacy of my research participants.

3. This song is a thematic song from the documentary film *The Red Flag Canal* (*hongqiqu* 红旗渠) (1970) that was produced by the Central Studio of News Reels Production of China. The original version for the excerpt above is as follows:

   劈开太行山,
   漳河穿山来,
   林县人民多奇志,
   誓把山河重安排!

4. The original verse for the translation above is:

   庄稼人为什么要识字?
   不识字不知道大事情,
   旧社会咱不识字,
   糊里糊涂受人欺。
   如今咱们翻了身,
   受苦人变成了当家的人,
   睁眼的瞎子怎能行?

Chapter 3

1. In 2020, I noticed, from the student recruitment guidelines of this education programme, that the restriction on learners with Haibin local household registers had been lifted.

References

Adedoyin, O. and E. Soykan (2020), 'Covid-19 Pandemic and Online Learning: The Challenges and Opportunities', *Interactive Learning Environments*, Advance online publication. DOI: 10.1080/10494820.2020.1813180.

All China Federation of Trade Unions (2010), '关于新生代 农民工问题的研究报告' (A research report on new generation rural-urban migrant workers). Available online: http://www.china-un.ch/chn/dbtyw/shbz_1/B_1/t711408.htm (accessed 12 February 2021).

Anagnost, A. (2004), 'The Corporeal Politics of Quality (Suzhi)', *Public Culture*, 16 (2): 189–208. DOI: https://doi.org/10.1215/08992363-16-2-189.

Ascher, I. (1976), *China's Social Policy*, London: Anglo-Chinese Educational Institute.

Barnett, R. (1997), 'A Knowledge Strategy for Universities', in R. Barnett and A. Griffin (eds.), *The End of Knowledge in Higher Education*, 166–79, London: Cassell.

Barthes, R. (1977), *Image Music Text*, trans. S. Heath, London: Fontana Press.

Bergsten, C., C. Freeman, N. Lardy and D. Mitchell (2009), *China's Rise: Challenges and Opportunities*, Washington: Peter G. Peterson Institute for International Economics.

Bogue, R. (1989), *Deleuze and Guattari*, London & New York: Routledge.

Bourdieu, P. and J. Passeron (1990), *Reproduction in Education, Society and Culture*, trans. R. Nice, 2nd edn, London, Thousand Oaks and New Delhi: Sage Publications.

Brødsgaard, K. and K. Rutten (2017), *From Accelerated Accumulation to the Socialist Market Economy in China: Economic Discourse and Development from 1953 to the Present*, Leiden and Boston: Brill.

Bryman, A. (2004), *Social Research Methods*, 2nd edn, Oxford: Oxford University Press.

Burgess, R. G. (1984), *In the Field: An Introduction to Field Research*, London: George Allen and Unwin.

Castles, S. and M. Miller (2009), *The Age of Migration: International Population Movements in the Modern World*, 4th edn, Basingstoke: Palgrave Macmillan.

Chen, M. (2014), '90后诗人许立志坠楼身亡' (Xu Lizhi died from falling from a building), 5th October, *Chengdu shangbao*. Available online: https://e.chengdu.cn/html/2014-10/05/content_491586.htm (accessed 22 February 2021).

Cheung, M. F. and W. Wu (2011), 'Participatory Management and Employee Work Outcomes: The Moderating Role of Supervisor–Subordinate Guanxi', *Asia Pacific Journal of Human Resources*, 49 (3): 344–64.

Cui, T. (2012), '新中国学徒制演变的制度分析' (Analysis of the changing system of apprenticeship in new China). Available online: http://www.xzbu.com/9/view-3058045.htm (accessed 2 February 2021).

DeLanda, M. (2004), 'Philosophy as Intensive Science', in H. Carel and D. Gamez (eds.), *What Philosophy Is*, 51–72, London and New York: Continuum.

Deleuze, G. and F. Guattari (1983), *Anti-Oedipus: Capitalism and Schizophrenia*, trans. R. Hurley, M. Seem and H. R. Lane, Minneapolis: Minnesota University Press.

Deleuze, G. and F. Guattari (1986), *Kafka: Towards a Minor Literature*, trans. D. Polan, Minneapolis: University of Minnesota Press.

Deleuze, G. and F. Guattari (1988), *A Thousand Plateaus: Capitalism and Schizophrenia*, trans. B. Massumi, London: Athlone Press.

Deleuze, G. and F. Guattari (1994), *What Is Philosophy?*, trans. H. Tomlinson and G. Burchell, New York: Columbia University Press.

Deleuze, G. and C. Parnet (1987), *Dialogues*, trans. H. Tomlinson and B. Habberjam, New York: Columbia University Press.

Du, L. (2016), 'Education, Social Stratification and Class', in Y. Guo (ed.), *Handbook on Class and Social Stratification in China*, 161–77, Cheltenham: Edward Elgar Publishing.

Education Committee of the PRC (1987), '国家教委1987年工作要点' (Education Committee of the PRC major tasks for 1987). Available online: http://www.moe.gov.cn/jyb_sjzl/moe_164/tnull_3450.html (accessed 22 February 2021).

Ellen, R. (ed.) (1984), *Ethnographic Research: A Guide to General Conduct*, London: Academic Press.

Emerson, J. (1983), 'Urban School-Leavers and Unemployment in China', *The China Quarterly*, 93: 1–16.

Escobar, A. (2007), 'Post-Development as Concept and Social Practice', in A. Ziai (ed.), *Exploring Post-Development: Theory and Practice, Problems and Perspectives*, 18–33, London and New York: Routledge.

Fetterman, D. M. (1998), *Ethnography: Step by Step*, Thousand Oaks, London and New Delhi: Sage Publications.

Gee, J. P. (1999), *An Introduction to Discourse Analysis Theory and Method*, 2nd edn, New York: Routledge.

Gold, T., D. Guthrie, and D. Wank (2002), 'An Introduction to the Study of Guanxi', in T. Gold, D. Guthrie and D. Wank (eds.), *Social Connections in China: Institution,*

Culture and the Changing Nature of Guanxi, 3–20, Cambridge: Cambridge University Press.

Gordon, C. (2020), 'Introduction', in (ed.), J. Faubion, (trans.), R. Hurley and others *Power: The Essential Works of Foucault 1954-1984*, XI–XLI, London: Penguin Books.

Gregory, B. and X. Meng (2018), 'Rural-to-Urban Migration and Migrants' Labour Market Performance 2008–16', in R. Garnaut, L. Song and C. Fang (eds*.), China's 40 Years of Reform and Development*, 395–426, Canberra: ANU Press.

Griffiths, M. B. and J. Zeuthen (2014), 'Bittersweet China: New Discourses of Hardship and Social Organisation', *Journal of Current Chinese Affairs*, 43 (4):143–74.

Grillo, R. D. (1997), 'Discourses of Development: The View from Anthropology', in R. D. Grillo and R. L. Stirrat (eds.), *Discourses of Development: Anthropological Perspectives*, 1–33, Oxford and New York: Berg.

Guo, X. L. (2017), '回忆当年扫文盲' (Recalling the then illiteracy elimination movement). Available online: http://www.linzhou.gov.cn:8090/Html/2017-05-23/10277.html (accessed 22 February 2021).

Hammersley, M. and P. Atkinson (2007), *Ethnography: Principles in Practice*, 3rd edn, New York: Routledge.

Hodgson, N. and P. Standish (2009), 'Uses and Misuses of Poststructuralism in Educational Research', *International Journal of Research & Method in Education*, 32 (3): 309–26.

Holmes, S. (2013), *Fresh Fruit, Broken Bodies: Migrant Farmworkers in the United States*, Berkeley, Los Angeles and London: University of California Press.

Jackson, C. (2006), 'Feminism Spoken Here: Epistemologies for Interdisciplinary Development Research', *Development and Change*, 37 (3): 525–47.

Kabeer, N. (1994), *Reversed Realities: Gender Hierarchies in Development Thought*, London and New York: Verso.

Kang, D. (2007), *China Rising: Peace, Power and Order in East Asia*, New York: Columbia University Press.

Kentli, F. (2009), 'Comparison of Hidden Curriculum Theories', *European Journal of Educational Studies*, 1 (2): 83–8.

Kelly, A. (2009), *The Curriculum: Theory and Practice*, London, Thousand Oaks and New Delhi: Sage Publications.

King, K. (1993), 'Technical and Vocational Education and Training in an International Context', *The Vocational Aspect of Education*, 45 (3): 201–16.

Kristeva, J. (1986), *The Kristeva Reader*, ed. T. Moi, New York: Columbia University Press.

Lardy, N. (1983), *Agriculture in China's Modern Economic Development*, Cambridge: Cambridge University Press.

Lebeau, Y. and A. Bennion (2014), 'Forms of Embeddedness and Discourses of Engagement: A Case Study of Universities in Their Local Environment', *Studies in Higher Education*, 39 (2): 278–93.

Li, C. (1960), 'Economic Development', *The China Quarterly*, 1 (Jan.–Mar.): 35–50.

Lie, J. (2008), 'Post-Development Theory and the Discourse-Agency Conundrum', *Social Analysis*, 52 (3): 118–37.

Lorraine, T. (1999), *Irigaray and Deleuze: Experiments in Visceral Philosophy*, Ithaca and London: Cornell University Press.

Lowe, J. (1999), 'International Examinations, National Systems and the Global Market', *Compare: A Journal of Comparative and International Education*, 29 (3): 317–30.

Loyalka, M. (2012), *Eating Bitterness: Stories from the Front Lines of China's Great Urban Migration*, Berkeley, Los Angeles and London: University of California Press.

Lytle, A. and S. Levy (2019), 'Reducing Ageism: Education about Aging and Extended Contact with Older Adults', *The Gerontologist*, 59 (3): 580–8.

Maclure, R., R. Sabbah and D. Lavan (2012), 'Education and Development: The Perennial Contradictions of Policy Discourse', in P. Haslam, J. Schafer and P. Beaudet (eds.), *Introduction to International Development: Approaches, Actors, and Issues*, 2nd edn, 399–414, Oxford: Oxford University Press.

Maitra, S. and S. Maitra (2018), 'Producing the Aesthetic Self: An Analysis of Aesthetic Skill and Labour in the Organized Retail Industries in India', *Journal of South Asian Development*, 13(3): 337–57.

Malinowski, B. ([1922] 2013), *Argonauts of the Western Pacific: An Account of Native Enterprise and Adventure in the Archipelagoes of Melanesian New Guinea*, Long Grove, IL: Waveland Press.

Mallee, H. (2000), 'Migration, Hukou and Resistance in Reform China', in E. Perry and M. Selden (eds.), *Chinese Society: Change, Conflict and Resistance*, 83–101, London and New York: Routledge.

Mao, Z. D. (1949), '在中国共产党第七届中央委员会第二次全体会议上的报告' (Report on the second plenary session of the seventh congress of CPC). Available online: http://www.yidan.net/plus/view.php?aid=725 (accessed 21 February 2021)

Mao, Z. D. (1957), '做革命的促进派' (Be an active revolutionary). Available online: http://news.xinhuanet.com/ziliao/2004-12/30/content_2397587.htm (accessed 21 February 2021).

Mao, Z. D. (1966), '五七指示', (May 7th Instructions). Available online: http://baike.baidu.com/view/60716.htm (accessed 21 February 2021).

Mao, Z. D. (1968), '毛主席语录' (Quotations from Chairman Mao), **人民日报** (People's Daily), 22 December. Available online: https://cn.govopendata.com/renminribao/1968/12/22/1/ (accessed 22 February 2021).

Marcus, G. E. and E. Saka (2006), 'Assemblage', *Theory, Culture & Society*, 23 (2–3): 101–9.

McNess, E., L. Arthur and M. Crossley (2013), '"Ethnographic Dazzle" and the Construction of the "Other": Revisiting Dimensions of Insider Outsider Research for International and Comparative Education', *Compare: A Journal of Comparative and International Research*, 45 (2): 295–316.

Ministry of Agriculture of PRC (2004), '关于组织实施农村劳动力转移培训阳光工程的通知', (Sunshine training project for rural labour force diversion). Available online: http://www.moa.gov.cn/gk/tzgg_1/tz/200403/t20040326_185530.htm (accessed 23 March 2021).

Ministry of Education of the PRC (2004), '教育部关于印发《农村劳动力转移培训计划》的通知'(Training plan for rural labour force diversion). Available online: http://www.moe.gov.cn/srcsite/A07/s7055/200403/t20040324_79140.html (accessed 23 March 2021).

Montenegro, C. and H. Patrinos (2013), 'Returns to Schooling around the World'. Available online: https://www.researchgate.net/publication/262602961_Returns_to_Schooling_around_the_World (accessed 22 February 2021).

Moore, M. (2012), ''Mass Suicide' Protest at Apple Manufacturer Foxconn Factory', *The Telegraph*, 11 January. Available online: http://www.telegraph.co.uk/news/worldnews/asia/china/9006988/Mass-suicide-protest-at-Apple-manufacturer-Foxconn-factory.html (accessed 21 February 2021).

Müller, M. and C. Schurr (2016), 'Assemblage Thinking and Actor-Network Theory: Conjunctions, Disjunctions, Cross-Fertilisations', *Transactions of the Institute of British Geographers*, 41 (3): 217–29.

Murphy, R. (2004), 'Turning Peasants into Modern Chinese Citizens: "Population Quality" Discourse, Demographic Transition and Primary Education', *The China Quarterly*, 177: 1–20.

National Bureau of Statistics of China (2010), '2009年农民工监测调查报告' (2009 Migrant workers' supervision and survey report). Available online: http://www.stats.gov.cn/tjfx/fxbg/t20100319_402628281.htm (accessed 21 February 2021).

National Health and Family Planning Commission of China (2013), '中国流动人口发展报告 2013 内容概要' (Summary of development report of floating population in China 2013). Available online: http://www.nhc.gov.cn/ldrks/s7847/201309/12e8cf0459de42c981c59e827b87a27c.shtml (accessed 16 January 2021).

National People's Congress of China (1954), *The Constitution of P.R. China*. Available online: http://www.npc.gov.cn/wxzl/wxzl/2000-12/26/content_4264.htm (accessed 28 March 2021).

NetEase (2013), '重庆化妆品公司让员工绕解放碑爬行' (A Chongqing Cosmetics Company trains employees to crawl). Available online: https://money.163.com/photoview/251H0025/8877.html?from=tj_xytj#p=8TT3J5CL251H0025 (accessed 28 March 2021).

Peterson, G. (2001), 'Peasant Education and Reconstruction of Village Society', in G. Peterson, R. Hayhoe and Y. Lu (eds.), *Education, Culture, and Identity in Twentieth-Century China*, Ann Arbor: University of Michigan Press.

Pi, J. (2018), '"共治"视角下新生代农民工职业教育机制研究' (Study on the vocational education mechanism of new generation migrant workers from the perspective of shared governance), *Journal of Zhejiang University of Technology (Social Science)*, 17 (3): 351–5.

Psacharopoulos, G. and H. Patrinos (2004), 'Returns to Investment in Education: A Further Update', *Education Economics*, 12 (2): 111–34. DOI: 10.1080/0964529042000239140.

Rao, N. and M. I. Hossain (2012), '"I Want to Be Respected": Migration, Mobility, and the Construction of Alternate Educational Discourses in Rural Bangladesh', *Anthropology and Education*, 43 (4): 415–28.

Robinson-Pant, A. (2000), *Why Eat Green Cucumbers at the Time of Dying?: Women's Literacy and Development in Nepal*, Hamburg: UNESCO Institute for Education.

Robinson-Pant, A. (2001), 'Development as Discourse: What Relevance to Education?' *Compare: A Journal of Comparative and International Research*, 31(3): 311–28.

Robinson-Pant, A. (2016), 'Exploring the Concept of Insider/Outsider in Comparative and International Research: Essentialising Culture or Culturally Essential?' in M. Croslley, L. Arthur and E. McNess (eds.), *Revisiting Insider–Outsider Research in Comparative and International Education, Bristol Papers in Education: Comparative and International Studies*, 39–55, Oxford: Symposium Books.

Rogers, A. (2014), *The Base of the Iceberg: Informal Learning and Its Impact on Formal and Non-formal Learning*, Opladen, Berlin and Toronto: Verlag Barbara Budrich.

State Council of China (1950), '政务院关于划分农村阶级成分的决定' (State Council of China's resolution on how to stratify rural classes). Available online: http://guoqing.china.com.cn/2012-09/03/content_26746212.htm (accessed 22 February 2021).

State Council of China (1951), '政务院关于改革学制的决定' (Resolution on reforming education system). Available online: https://cn.govopendata.com/renminribao/1951/10/3/1/ (accessed 23 February 2022).

State Council of China (1956), '关于扫除文盲的决定' (The Notice on Illiteracy Elimination). Available online: https://cn.govopendata.com/renminribao/1956/3/31/1/ (accessed 8 March 2021).

State Council of China (2003), '*2003–2010* 年全国农民工培训规划' (2003–2010 China's rural-urban migrant workers training plan). Available online: http://www.gov.cn/zwgk/2005-08/14/content_22484.htm (accessed 19 February 2021).

State Council of China (2006), '国务院关于解决农民工问题的若干意见' (Some guidelines of State Council on how to solve the problems of the rural-urban migrant workers). Available online: http://www.gov.cn/gongbao/content/2006/content_244909.htm (accessed 18 February 2021).

State Council of China (2008), '国务院办公厅关于切实做好当前农民工工作的通知' (Notice of State Council of China on solidification of current migrant workers' affairs). Available online: http://www.gov.cn/zwgk/2008-12/20/content_1183721.htm (accessed 19 February 2021).

State Council of China (2010), '国务院办公厅关于进一步做好农民工培训工作的指导意见' (State Council of China guidelines for further training of migrant workers). Available online: http://www.gov.cn/zwgk/2010-01/25/content_1518915.htm (accessed 16 February 2021).

Street, B. V. (1984), *Literacy in Theory and Practice*, Cambridge and New York: Cambridge University Press.

Street, B. V. (2003), 'What's "New" in New Literacy Studies? Critical Approaches to Literacy in Theory and Practice', *Current Issues in Comparative Education*, 5 (2): 77–91. Available online: https://www.tc.columbia.edu/cice/pdf/25734_5_2_Street.pdf (accessed 31 March 2021).

Street, B. V. (2011), 'Literacy Inequalities in Theory and Practice: The Power to Name and Define', *International Journal of Educational Development*, 31 (6): 580–6.

Sun, J. and M. Hao (2019), '中国的高考如何改变许多人的命运?' (How university entrance exams changed many people's fates?) 7 October. Available online: http://politics.people.com.cn/n1/2019/1007/c429373-31385971.html (accessed 8 March 2021).

Sun, W. (2020), 'Rural Migrant Workers in Chinese Cities', in K. Latham (ed.), *Routledge Handbook of Chinese Culture and Society*, 115–28, Oxon and New York: Routledge.

UNESCO (2015), *EDUCATION FOR ALL 2000–2015: Achievements and Challenges, EFA Global Monitoring Report*. Available online: https://unesdoc.unesco.org/ark:/48223/pf0000232205 (accessed 22 February 2021).

UNESCO Institute for Lifelong Learning (2020), *Embracing a Culture of Lifelong Learning: Contribution to the Futures of Education Initiative Report*.

Available online: https://uil.unesco.org/lifelong-learning/embracing-culture-lifelong-learning (accessed 18 March 2021).

Vlachopoulos, D. (2020), 'COVID-19: Threat or Opportunity for Online Education?' ***Higher Learning Research Communication***, 10 (1): 16–19. DOI: 10.18870/hlrc.v10i1.1179

Wacquant, L. (2003), 'Ethnografeast: A Progress Report on the Practice and Promise of Ethnography', ***Ethnography***, 4 (1): 5–14.

Warner, M. (1986), 'Managing Human Resources in China: An Empirical Study', ***Organization Studies***, 7 (4): 353–66.

Wang, G. (1989), 'The Basic Tasks of China's First Five-Year Plan', in C. Howe and K. Walker (eds.), ***The Foundations of the Chinese Planned Economy: A Documentary Survey 1953–65***, Basingstoke: Macmillan.

Wang, L. and W. Chen (2021), '加速城镇化背景下进城农民工职业培训问题研究' (A study of the vocational training of migrant workers in the context of accelerating urbanization)', ***产业与科技论坛*** (Industrial and Science Tribune), 18: 63–64.

Wang, X. and Y. Zhang (2015), '新学徒 徒弟与师傅是合同关系' (New apprenticeships as contracted relationship between master workers and apprentices). Available online: http://cpc.people.com.cn/n/2015/0907/c83084-27550291.html (accessed 28 March 2021).

Wen, J. (2004), '从分治到融合:近五十年来我国劳动力移民制度的演变及其影响' (From segregation to integration: Evolution and influence of China's migrant systems of labour force in the last 50 years)', ***学术研究*** (Academic research), 7: 32–6.

Wen, J. B. (2009), 'Premier Wen Jiabao Talks to the Financial Times', ***Beijing Review***, 1st February. Available online: http://www.bjreview.com.cn/document/txt/2009-02/24/content_179988_2.htm (accessed 22 February 2021).

Wong, D., C. Y. Li and H. X. Song (2007), 'Rural Migrant Workers in Urban China: Living a Marginalised Life', ***International Journal of Social Welfare***, 16 (1): 32–40.

Wright, S. and N. Nelson (1995), 'Participatory Research and Participant Observation: Two Incompatible Approaches', in N. Nelson and S. Wright (eds.), ***Power and Participatory Development: Theory and Practice***, 43–59, London: ITP.

Wu, H. (1994), 'Rural to Urban Migration in the People's Republic of China', ***The China Quarterly***, 139: 669–98.

Xi, J. P. (2012), '实现中华民族伟大复兴的中国梦' (Realising the Chinese dream of great rejuvenation of the Chinese nation). Available online: http://cpc.people.com.cn/xuexi/n/2015/0717/c397563-27322292.html (accessed 16 April 2021).

Xi, J. P. (2013a), '让人民共享人生出彩的机会' (Let the people share the glory of human life). Available online: http://news.sina.com.cn/c/2013-03-18/023926559533.shtml (accessed 22 February 2021).

Xi, J. P. (2013b), '美好梦想只有通过诚实劳动才能实现', (Beautiful dream can be realized only through honest labour). Available online: https://news.qq.com/a/20130429/000088.htm (accessed 22 February 2021).

Xi, J. P. (2017), '决胜全面建成小康社会 夺取新时代中国特色社会主义伟大胜利' (Constructing a well-off society and winning the victory of socialism with Chinese characteristics). Available online: http://www.gov.cn/zhuanti/2017-10/27/content_5234876.htm (accessed 22 February 2021).

Xi, J. P. (2020), '在教育文化卫生体育领域专家代表座谈会上的讲话' (A speech on the conference for representatives of the experts in education, culture, healthcare and sports). Available online: http://www.moe.gov.cn/jyb_xwfb/moe_176/202009/t20200923_489988.html (accessed 7 March 2021).

Xinhua Agency (1956), '庆祝社会主义改造完成' (Celebration on the completion of socialist reform), 7 August. Available online: http://www.gov.cn/test/2009-08/07/content_1385567.htm (accessed 28 March 2021).

Xu, L. Z. '我像流水线一样辛苦的光阴' (Lost time, toilsome as assembly lines). Availableonline:https://wenku.baidu.com/view/85608ef88ad63186bceb19e8b8f67c1cfad6eeb2.html?re=view# (accessed 22 February 2021).

Yan, H. R. (2008), *New Masters, New Servants: Migration, Development, and Women Workers in China*, Durham and London: Duke University Press.

Yee, H. (ed.) (2011), *China's Rise – Threat or Opportunity?*, London and New York: Routledge.

Yi, S. (2019), '从扫除文盲到教育强国' (From illiteracy elimination to a country of strong education). Available online: http://www.moe.gov.cn/jyb_xwfb/s5147/201909/t20190924_400598.html (accessed 22 February 2021).

Zeng, R., X. Jia and Y. He (2009), '流动人口继续教育的影响及其对策分析' (Factors influencing continuing education of migrants and their countermeasures), 成人教育 (Adult Education) (6): 14–16.

Zhang, S., Y. Ding and Y. Wu (2021), '恢复高考,知识改变中国' (Resuming university entrance exams: Knowledge changed China), 人民日报 (The People's Daily), 26 February. Available online: http://paper.people.com.cn/rmrb/html/2021-02/26/nw.D110000renmrb_20210226_1-06.htm (accessed 8 March 2021).

Zhao, Y. (2002) 'The Rich, the Laid-off, and the Criminal in Tabloid Tales: Read All About Them!' in P. Link, R. P. Madsen and P. G. Pickowicz (eds.), *Popular China: Unofficial Culture in a Globalizing Society*, 111–36, Lanham, MD: Rowman and Littlefield.

Index

absenteeism 93–4, 111–12
adult learning 2–3, 11–16, 18, 27, 36, 43, 49, 60, 109, 131, 133, 141–3, 145, 149, 161–2, 169, 175
   affectivity 152–5
   attitudes 143–9
   enterprise culture 149–51
   knowledge and fate 135–41
   multiple modes and accreditation 155–60
   and social change 167–8
   social connections 141–3
   subject formulation 134–5
   underlying rules 142
affect 39, 102, 126, 130, 152–5, 167
All-China Federation of Trade Unions (2010) 10
Anti-Oedipus: Capitalism and Schizophrenia (Deleuze and Guattari) 150
Arthur, L. 30–1, 35
Ascher, I. 12
asignifying rupture 39, 55, 57, 82, 147
aspiration 2, 17, 27, 31, 84, 92, 131, 133–6, 140, 141, 143, 151, 161, 164, 167, 171, 175
assemblage 26, 38–40, 43, 48, 55, 57, 67, 69, 74, 77, 79, 86, 100, 102, 108, 114, 116, 122, 123, 131, 134, 135, 139, 147, 149–51, 161, 163–7, 174–6
Atkinson, P. 40
attendance registration 25, 26, 85, 90–4, 100
autonomous model 140

Barnett, R. 140, 170
Beijing Lakeview University 18, 57, 58, 62, 63
Beijing Skyline University 25, 48, 77, 87, 117, 119, 123
Bennion, A. 63, 170
Bogue, R. 36, 134

Bourdieu, P. 72, 115, 116, 126, 130, 142, 161
Bryman, A. 19
Burgess, R. G. 36

Chen Yi 24, 85, 92, 93, 118, 126
Cheung, M. F. 64
China 1, 4
   literacy 11, 12
   social development 82–3
Chinese Dream 47–8, 91, 94, 100, 162
Chuan Aixiang 62, 69, 86, 87, 160
Class of Economic Management 81, 88, 92, 93, 98, 106, 109, 111, 119, 150
Class of Machinery Engineering 112, 119, 128, 138
class struggle 5–7, 14
collectivism 3, 5, 27, 82, 100, 101, 112–14, 170, 171, 173
commercialism/commercialization 2–3, 26, 27, 60, 71, 84, 100, 103, 112–14, 130, 155, 169–71
conscientization 175
contingency 39
Covid-19 pandemic 3, 101, 102, 144, 164, 174
Crossley, M. 30–1, 35
Cui, T. 11
curriculum 40, 44, 94, 170, 173
   college 112, 113
   didactic 86, 95
   hidden 86, 100, 116
   and pedagogical practice 100–3
   total 49, 106, 110, 169
   unwritten 86, 95, 100–3
   written 100–3

DeLanda, M. 90
Deleuze, G. 38, 39, 55, 82, 83, 86, 90, 102, 108, 122, 123, 134, 135, 147, 150, 161, 162, 165, 166, 169, 176
Deng Xiaoping 4, 7

development as discourse 26, 36–8, 40, 43, 108, 165, 169
digital technologies 2, 19, 86, 89–90, 101, 102, 121, 163, 168
Dream Fulfilment Plan 17, 18
Du, L. 167

Economic Management Class 24, 25, 48, 59, 61, 77, 85, 88, 114, 117, 123, 124, 128
Educated Youth Urban-Rural Migration 6
education
  policies 43–55, 70–2
  practitioners 17, 26, 43, 55–60, 63, 71, 131, 143, 172, 173
EFA Global Monitoring Report 101
enterprise culture 149–51
Escobar, A. 108, 111, 119
ethnography 2, 3, 18–25, 29, 31–6, 39–41, 175

face-to-face teaching 22, 25, 26, 82, 86–8, 90, 94, 101–3, 110, 123, 124, 173
Fang Xu 37, 160
Feng Jun 52, 65, 155, 159, 161
Fetterman, D. M. 24, 32
First Five Year Plan 4
'Five Evil Types' 6, 14
formal learning 27, 67, 70, 137, 138, 147–9, 157–61, 167, 171
Foucault, M. 82, 134, 150, 169
Foxconn Group 52, 165, 166
funding
  resources 26, 56–8, 60, 77, 122
  support 67–70

Gaokao 14
Grillo, R. D. 120, 143
Guangdong Province 8
Guattari, F. 38, 39, 55, 82, 83, 123, 134, 147, 149, 150, 161, 162, 165, 166, 169
Guo, X. L. 12

Haibin General Trade Union 18, 23, 44–6, 56, 57, 61, 64, 91, 136
Haibin Trade Union 23, 57, 91
Haibin Yuanmeng Plan 18, 22, 23, 32, 33, 36, 40, 43, 45–51, 53–6, 58, 59, 61, 62, 64, 65, 70, 77, 85, 86, 89, 91, 92, 94, 100, 127, 129, 133, 135, 136, 144, 146, 147, 150, 151, 163, 164, 169–71
Hammersley, M. 40
handwritten reference materials 116–18
hegemony 94, 127
heterogeneity 27, 38–40, 43, 48, 55, 60, 86, 90, 122, 134, 139, 140, 155, 163, 164, 175
He, Y. 50, 71
higher education 1, 13–18, 50, 60, 62, 63, 77, 101, 102, 140, 170
Hodgson, N. 134, 137
Holmes, S. 8
Home of Migrants College 23–7, 29–34, 37, 44–6, 48, 49, 56, 58–9, 61, 70, 71, 73–83, 85–95, 97–101, 103, 105–8, 110, 113–18, 121–3, 125–30, 133, 135–7, 143, 144, 170, 172, 173
Hossain, M. I. 157
hukou system 5, 8, 50, 53, 70, 71

ideological model 140
informal learning 3, 27, 123, 137, 138, 149, 156, 157, 159–61, 171, 172
insider/outsider dualism 35–6
interactive teaching 26, 31, 85, 95, 98, 99, 101, 103, 114, 170
internet 87, 89, 101, 118
interworld 36, 40, 64, 102

Jiang Danian 13
Jia, X. 50, 71
job advertisement 51, 68, 138, 153, 159
'just in case' 143–5

Kabeer, N. 8, 52, 61, 65, 66, 70, 73, 122, 139, 157, 165, 175
Kelly, A. 49, 99, 127
Kentli, F. 94
King, K. 174
knowledge 36, 37, 133, 168–71
'knowledge changes fate' 27, 133, 135–41, 144, 164, 171

Lao Yang 66, 67
laziness 145–7

learners response
  excellent employees 61–2
  funding support 67–70
  Lychee Waterfront University 62–4
  social relations 64–6
learning. *See also* adult learning
  attitudes 143–9
  enthusiasm 12, 32
  formal 27, 67, 70, 137, 138, 147–9, 157–61, 167, 171
  informal 3, 27, 123, 137, 138, 149, 156, 157, 159–61, 171, 172
  non-formal 138, 157, 159–61, 172
  online 102, 103, 123, 127, 172, 173
Lebeau, Y. 63, 170
Levy, S. 52
Liang, C. 17, 102
Li, C. Y. 8, 11
literacy 10–15, 46, 53–5, 69, 71, 125, 140, 141, 144, 147, 168
Liu Qiang 119, 120, 128, 138, 142, 147, 171
Li Wenhua 13
Li Ying 75, 95, 136–8, 141–6, 148
Long Guozheng 13, 14
Lorrain, T. 134
Lowe, J. 130, 170
Loyalka, M. 1
Lychee City 18–23, 51–4, 57, 59, 62, 63, 69, 70, 73, 77, 79, 87, 152, 153, 155, 156, 158–60
Lychee Municipal Government 79, 87
Lychee Seabreeze Academy 22, 58, 87, 174
Lychee Waterfront University 21, 22, 57, 59, 62–4, 70, 77–9, 83, 87, 169
Lytle, A. 52

Machinery Engineering Class 24, 25, 77, 89, 106, 112, 114, 117, 119, 123, 128, 138, 147
McNess, E. 30–1, 35
Malinowski, B. 29, 41
Mao Zedong 5–6, 9, 12, 13, 82
Marcus, G. E. 39
migration
  prior knowledge of 36–40
  state policies and 4–10
Ministry of Education 15
mock test designs 118–21
Montenegro, C. 162

multiplicity 38, 39, 122, 135, 155, 162, 165
Murphy, R. 16

naturalized suffering 8, 9
negotiations 27, 29, 31–3, 57, 63, 69, 76, 90, 107, 112, 118, 122, 126, 130, 131, 161, 174
Nelson, N. 30
non-formal learning 138, 157, 159–61, 172
nongmingong (peasant workers) 7, 9, 37, 44
noteworthy 55, 71, 123, 130

online learning 102, 103, 123, 127, 172, 173
outward development 27, 105–14, 123, 129, 151
  absenteeism 111–12
  collectivism 113–14
  commercialism 112–14
  university life 109–11

Passeron, J. 72, 115, 116, 126, 130, 161
Patrinos, H. 162
patriotism 3, 92, 100, 171
Pearl River Delta 8, 50
pedagogical practice 76, 85–6
  attendance registration 90–4
  curriculum and 100–3
  'interaction' 94–9
  virtual spaces and actual spaces 86–90
Peng Zhen 4
People's Republic of China 3–5, 11, 152
Pi, J. 16–17
plane 39, 55, 122, 155, 166
policy makers 26, 43, 62, 63, 70, 71, 169, 172–6
political mobilizations 11–14
population quality 10, 15, 16
positionality 25, 29, 110
primary school education 137
processes 35–6
Psacharopoulos, G. 162

QQ chat room 53, 58, 59, 62, 109, 111, 123, 124
quitting 147–9

Rao, N. 157
reciprocity 24, 32

Red Flag Canal 6
reflexivity 3, 26, 30-1, 33, 36
researcher and researched 33-4
Robinson-Pant, A. 34, 35, 38, 49, 147
Rogers, A. 149, 159
rural-urban migration 4, 5, 9, 31

Saka, E. 39
Shu Li 156-9, 161
social connections 141-3
socialism 3, 8, 49, 71, 100, 171
socialist market economy 7-9
Social Relations Framework 26, 30, 36,
    38-40, 43, 56, 60, 64-6, 70, 73-4,
    118, 122, 126, 134, 141, 142, 165
Song, H. X. 8
Standish, P. 134, 137
State Council of China 9, 11, 15, 16
Street, B. V. 46, 140
student recruitment 14, 21, 47, 50-5,
    58-60, 70, 71, 80, 113, 114, 169, 170
students assessment 115-16, 130-1
    expectations 128-9
    handwritten reference materials
        116-18
    interactive social process 121-7
    mock test 118-21
subjectivities 26, 29, 30, 38, 55, 82, 140,
    165, 167
    ever-changing and nomadic 161-2,
        176
    formulation of 134-5, 139
    of researcher 40-1
suffering (*shou*) 8
supplementary rules 85, 91, 94, 99, 116,
    118
sympathy 31, 38, 123, 130, 153

Taiyuan City 4, 5, 7, 14
teaching force 26, 73-4, 83-4
    ideological consistency 77-9
    local 76
    'our own staff' and the external 74-7
    'working hard' 79-83
teamwork spirit 80-3, 118, 120, 149
tensions and contradictions 169-72
textbook 116-18, 128, 146
top-down programmes 168
training lecturers 73, 81, 82, 99

underlying rules 142
UNESCO 3, 53, 102, 113, 160, 172
university education 14, 15, 109-11, 131, 173

Wacquant, L. 19
wailaigong 9, 53
'Wall Street' 98-9
Wang, L. 17, 102
Wang Shaogang 56, 74-6, 80, 81, 91, 94,
    95, 97, 110, 116, 117, 122, 124-5,
    127-9, 143
Warner, M. 152
Wei Jie 154, 156, 157, 159
Wen Xiangyang 29, 89, 163
Wong, D. 8
Wright, S. 30
Wu, W. 64
Wu Xiaohong 135-7, 139, 141

Xiao Zhiyuan 23, 24, 32, 33, 56, 80, 85,
    125, 133
Xi Jinping 3, 10, 47, 52, 100, 162, 171
Xu Lizhi 2, 166

Yangtse River Delta 8
Yin Fa 32, 158-9, 161, 162, 166
Yuanda Communist Youth League 18, 64,
    77, 78
Yuanda Province 2, 3, 17-19, 21, 22, 26,
    43, 45, 46, 49, 53, 54, 57, 58, 74, 77,
    91, 115, 138, 147, 149, 152, 163,
    167, 169, 172, 175
Yuanda Yuanmeng Plan 18, 19, 21, 22,
    30, 32, 40, 43-7, 49-51, 53-9, 62,
    63, 69, 73, 77, 79, 86, 87, 116, 164,
    169, 172
Yuanmeng education programmes 167
Yuanmeng plans 44-6, 60, 63, 67, 71, 72,
    83, 84, 90, 91, 105, 163, 164, 168-73
    mainstream discourse 47-8
    student recruitment rules 50-5
    utilitarian projects 49-50

Zeng, R. 50, 71
Zhang Li 136, 137, 139-42, 168, 171
Zhang Xiaohu 53-4, 65-7, 69, 71, 141, 168
Zhao Daming 24, 59, 79, 81-3, 85, 92, 107,
    109, 111, 112
Zhou Li 24, 85, 88, 116, 118, 125

www.ingramcontent.com/pod-product-compliance
Lightning Source LLC
Chambersburg PA
CBHW061831300426
44115CB00013B/2339